If secularization looks like the illegitimate child of Christianity, then its parent has shown itself singularly incapable of coping with the tests and trials presented to it by its offspring. In *The Exiled Church*, Martyn Percy puts this relationship in the spotlight. He offers a persuasively written analysis that is, by turns, challenging and perplexing, yet also offering glimmers of hope – or at least hope for hope.

The Revd Professor Stephen Morgan, Rector,
University of Saint Joseph, Macao

Anyone knowing Martyn Percy's work will already realize that he is habitually averse to applying saccharine, romanticism or institutionalism to his subjects. This deep dive into today's church is no exception. In a world suffering from what he calls 'truth decay', Percy's analysis is not afraid of reality. Much of the data is frankly frightening. Drilling into attendance figures, finance and the distribution of power exposes a bleak landscape, and yet this book is not without hope. Religion is not dead, it's just not where you think it is any more.

The Revd Canon Rosie Harper

Martyn Percy is reliably incisive, well-read and creative. The Christian churches in their many varieties are undergoing accelerating decline if not crisis. This short, provocative book offers a curriculum in reorientation. Historically, exile has been a time of vitality. He disentangles statistics, sociologies and trends to show how much of the hollowing out of the churches has been self-inflicted. Ideologies are adopted as values as if they were matters of faith, and unaccountable officials have sheltered behind 'canon law'.

Professor Sir Iain Torrance, President Emeritus,
Princeton Theological Seminary

Martyn Percy deploys his formidable talent and long experience on the central challenge for the modern church: how to define its role in a society that seems to have cast it out. He is a model teacher, keen to correct but unfailingly humane, reasonable and encouraging. His perspective is simultaneously broad and eagle-eyed; there are fascinating insights on every page, with ideas that could and should fuel weeks of discussion in a book group and years of debate within the church.

Emeritus Professor David Voas, University College London

This is a compelling and creative book by Martyn Percy in which he skilfully leads readers to understand the potency and potential 'heresy' of secularization within the churches. Percy uses the model of a school curriculum to explore secularization in many areas of study, drawing important implications and insights for religion. He presents a sophisticated revisionist account of the future of the churches which heightens the role of religion in the present. Another outstanding work by an accomplished scholar and thinker which assists the church in heading into the future.

The Revd Professor Brian Douglas,
Australian Centre for Christianity and Culture,
Editor, The Journal of Anglican Studies

A hugely enjoyable book, which reads very smoothly, even if its message is challenging, especially for those who are part of the institutional church. What Percy writes about the Church of England equally applies to the Roman Catholic Church as I experience it in Belgium. The modern Christian heresy of secularization is rampant in our churches. Not only does it feed ecclesial self-secularization, but it prevents them from seeing the new ways in which religion takes shape in society today, not to mention hampering our churches' ability to learn from it and deal with it in humility and humanity. As Martyn Percy rightly claims, only God's mercy and grace can save them now. In the meantime, reading this unconventional and thought-provoking book will be of great help.

Professor Lieven Boeve, KU Leuven (Leuven University)

Anyone knowing Martyn Percy's work will already realize that he is habitually averse to applying saccharine, romanticism or institutionalism to his subjects. This deep dive into today's church is no exception. In a world suffering from what he calls 'truth decay', Percy's analysis is not afraid of reality. Much of the data is frankly frightening. Drilling into attendance figures, finance and the distribution of power exposes a bleak landscape, and yet this book is not without hope. Religion is not dead, it's just not where you think it is any more.

The Revd Canon Rosie Harper, Oxford

The Church is haemorrhaging both people and credibility. Part of the reason for this stems from broader social and cultural changes, but as much appears to be the product of self-harm. Scandal follows scandal and mistrust becomes distrust. Church 'messaging' increasingly has the feel (and all the depth) of a PR reputation management programme, but to little avail. In *The Exiled Church*, Martyn Percy has written a tremendous book to goad and guide the honest and soul-searching conversations that will be essential if the church is not to bleed out the trust which is its very lifeblood.

Dr Andrew McKinnon, University of Aberdeen

In his characteristically astute and engaging style, the Very Revd Professor Martyn Percy explores current and future institutionalized Christianity and its relationship with secularity. Written for religious professionals who may be unfamiliar with secularization theory and practice, Percy designs the book around 'lessons' meant to inform and prepare Church leaders for the dark period ahead. Through brave and unflinching analysis, delivered often with a light touch, Percy both criticizes and challenges leaders whose states of denial are responsible for the Church's self-secularizing decline. Proponents of secularization theory also have lessons to learn, he says, advising them to recognize how the profane and sacred can overlap and mutually infuse.

Unlike most priests and theologians, Percy treats respectfully secular professionals who are non-religious, yet often spiritual and 'implicitly religious'. Those 'agony aunts' and therapists who offer the weary and heavy-laden the compassion, hope and grace one might have expected from a Church, now almost wholly self-centred and distracted by ambitions of growth and false gods of marketing and managerialism.

Only in exile, and banking on a forgiving God, can Christian leaders accept their inevitable societal expulsion as a blessing, not a curse. He urges them to see that period as an opportunity to reflect, pray and learn their lessons. While, one assumes, avoiding stony ground.

Professor Emeritus Abby Day, Goldsmiths, University of London

The Exiled Church

Reckoning with Secular Culture

Martyn Percy

CANTERBURY
PRESS

© Martyn Percy 2025

First published in 2025 by the Canterbury Press Norwich

Editorial office
3rd Floor, Invicta House
110 Golden Lane
London EC1Y 0TG, UK
www.canterburypress.co.uk

Canterbury Press is an imprint of Hymns Ancient & Modern Ltd
(a registered charity)

Hymns Ancient & Modern® is a registered trademark of
Hymns Ancient & Modern Ltd
13A Hellesdon Park Road, Norwich,
Norfolk NR6 5DR, UK

All rights reserved. No part of this publication may be reproduced,
stored in a retrieval system, or transmitted,
in any form or by any means, electronic, mechanical,
photocopying or otherwise, without the prior permission of
the publisher, Canterbury Press.

The Author has asserted his right under the Copyright, Designs and
Patents Act 1988 to be identified as the Author of this Work

Scripture quotations are from

the New Revised Standard Version Bible: Anglicized Edition, copyright © 1989,
1995 National Council of the Churches of Christ in the United States of America.
Used by permission. All rights reserved worldwide.

the Authorized Version of the Bible (The King James Bible), the rights in which
are vested in the Crown, are reproduced by permission of the Crown's Patentee,
Cambridge University Press.

the ESV Bible (The Holy Bible, English Standard Version), copyright © 2001
by Crossway, a publishing ministry of Good News Publishers.
Used by permission. All rights reserved.

British Library Cataloguing in Publication data

A catalogue record for this book is available
from the British Library

ISBN: 978 1 78622 627 3

EU GPSR Authorised Representative
LOGOS EUROPE, 9 rue Nicolas Poussin, 17000, LA ROCHELLE, France
E-mail: Contact@logoseurope.eu

Typeset by Regent Typesetting

Contents

Acknowledgements   v

Introduction: Syllabus   1
Terms of Reference: Secularization   13
From the Development Office: Change in the Faith Markets   23
Opening Assembly: Inclusive and Impartial   33

Lesson One:	Maths	37
Lesson Two:	Geography	47
Lesson Three:	History	55
Lesson Four:	Languages	65
Lesson Five:	Design and Technology	75
Half Term:	Extra Maths and Equations	83
Lesson Six:	Science	97
Lesson Seven:	Politics and Economics	107
Lesson Eight:	Religious Education	117
Lesson Nine:	Sport and Leisure	127
Lesson Ten:	Cultural and Moral Education	135

Governance: Leadership in Managing Diversity   143
Report: From the Counselling Service   153
Term Ends: Closing Assembly and Farewells   161
Future Directions: what3words? Go, Make, Disciples   169
Prospects: Onwards and Upwards?   179
From the Librarian: References and Further Reading   187

Acknowledgements

Thanks to the McDonald Agape Foundation, the Rannoch Trust and the Farmington Institute for all their support in this work during 2023–24. During that time, I was privileged to serve as Dean's Distinguished Scholar at Virginia Theological Seminary for the 2023–24 academic year, and I wish to particularly thank the Very Revd Dr Ian Markham, its Dean and President, for his generous hosting and munificent hospitality. Likewise, to friends and colleagues from the Anglican Province of Hong Kong and Macao and Ming Hua Theological College staff. I owe them all a huge debt of gratitude. I also wish to thank my friends and colleagues at the University of Saint Joseph in Macao, especially the Revd Professor Stephen Morgan. The same is so for friends and colleagues at Institut für Christkatholische Theologie, Theologische Fakultät, Universität Bern, CH, and especially Professor Angela Berlis. This book would, of course, not have been possible without the unstinting support of the publisher, and I want to especially thank Christine Smith for her fine direction and oversight, and Mary Matthews and Hannah Ward for their assistance.

I also wish to thank all those 'on the ground' (so to speak) during the gathering of the material for the book and who provided insights, data, conversation and analysis that helped in the gestation of this book. There are far too many to mention by name, but I want to record my appreciation and thanks to them for their time, wisdom and refreshing discernment.

Last but by no means least, this project has been helped enormously and richly sustained in conversations with Emma over many years. While it is not surprising that our interests, passions and concerns are often aligned, love delights in revealing afresh that two heads are better than one (Ecclesiastes 4.9–12) and that a cord of three strands – faith, hope and love – cannot easily be broken.

MWP, Epiphany 2025

Introduction: Syllabus

As an eager young curate over 30 years ago, I was assigned by the vicar to take Confirmation classes for the youth group. These classes met late on Sunday afternoons every week for a few months or more. A group of around 20 young teenagers would squeeze into the main living room of our house, and we would talk about faith, church, belief – and what was good and bad on TV. The classes culminated in the Confirmation service, presided over by the local bishop.

With other smaller churches feeding in candidates young and old, as many as 40 people might be confirmed in one service, the vast majority of whom were youngsters. The bishop would walk along the aisle, laying hands upon each kneeling candidate, blessing them and confirming them in their adult profession of Christian faith before they received Holy Communion for the first time. Parents, grandparents, siblings and godparents swelled the congregation to bursting point.

These moving occasions marked the younger candidates' transition from childhood to adulthood. For older candidates, this was something else. Some had returned to faith after a lengthy lacuna. Others had come from Christian traditions that they had moved on from or, in some cases, had been expelled from because of their beliefs. Others had attended church faithfully all their lives yet had never been confirmed, and this was their way of preparing for death.

There is no prescribed syllabus for Confirmation classes – at least in the Church of England. Today, some might use Alpha as a basis for delivering them. Others turned to courses from Pilgrim, but without any internet to rely on, we were left to construct classes from books, manuals, booklets and other resources. This being the Church of England, neighbouring parish clergy in the town all took different approaches. Evangelical clergy used the writings of John Stott, with a nod towards David Watson. The more Anglo-Catholic clergy could roll out the *Catholic Catechism* or some other publication from the Catholic

Truth Society that stressed the sacramental nature of Confirmation. Our church, situated between these two polarities, was largely left to its own devices.

Explaining Christian faith to folk who already know a bit about it is not that difficult. What is challenging, however, is making it interesting, engaging, relevant, challenging and inspiring for young teenagers. Well, we tried our best. And more than 30 years on, many remain churchgoers. But one lesson sticks in my mind particularly. It was a bit of homework set for the group: to go away in pairs, think about the best or most exciting parable Jesus had taught, and explain next week to their peers why they'd chosen it and how it inspired them to practise their faith and live.

One pair returned the following week and proudly announced their favourite was Jesus' Parable of the Chopsticks. Momentarily, I thought they might be pulling my leg. So, I asked the pair to explain. The parable, it seems, involved the difference between heaven and hell, but each place is equipped with chopsticks (other versions have very long spoons). It holds that the inhabitants are given access to food in heaven and hell, but the utensils are too unwieldy to serve themselves. In hell, the people will not cooperate, so consequently starve. In heaven, the diners feed one another and are sated. The story is intended to encourage people to help and be kind to one another and is often attributed to a well-known Latvian rabbi, Haim of Romshishok.

Hopefully, readers of this book will immediately realize that Jesus never 'spake' the Parable of the Chopsticks or its variant using extra-long spoons. True, there is nothing wrong with the parable, per se. It carries a message about caring for one another rather than simply trying to look after your interests to the exclusion of others. Naturally, I asked the pair where they had got the parable from, and it turned out to be a story from one of the school assemblies that had moved them and left its mark. Any good teacher (or, for that matter, curate) would recognize the excellent intention at work in the story and its repetition and work with that. We did.

However, some churchgoers might despair at this anecdote and see it as part of a more comprehensive set of crises. The decline in religious literacy and the growing problem of ignorance might be one concern. Another concerned churchgoer might attribute this anecdote to society's inherent secularization. Some would blame the schooling, others the parents, and others the church.

'Secular' is a peculiar term used to base an entire premise. Like 'plague', 'epidemic' and 'disease', the terms strike fear in the heart and cause widespread panic. In truth, few of these conditions are fatal, and as pathologists who study disease will confirm, many afflictions are mild, natural, normal and hardly severe. 'Secular' has come to mean non-religious, but for some it will suggest the promotion of profane, godless, pagan and atheistic values. It need not mean this. As pathologists remind us, disease is normal and natural. The question is, what potency and potential does it carry?

'Secular' entered our vocabulary quite early. It originally referred to clergy in medieval times who were not part of a religious order but lived and ministered in the world. On that definition alone, nearly all Anglican and Protestant clergy would qualify as 'secular'. More broadly, the term drew from Latin and Greek roots and was concerned with temporality, ages, eras, generations and lifespan. The secular was not eternal. But it did *breed*, and its other etymological roots tie it to seeds and sowing (as with our word 'seminary'), binding and tying (from which we get our word 'religion'), and 'epoch' (referring to something that might take place once in a generation or century, or last for some lengthy period).

Based on this reading of the term 'secular', it is hard to think of any era in Christian history that has not been exposed to some form of secularization. The separation of religion from broader society and the sacred from the profane are, after all, issues for writers of the New Testament, as much as they impacted the early church. 'Secular' is perfectly normal and natural. And interestingly, not necessarily non-religious, as we shall see. Christians must begin to understand the potency and potential of the secular within their churches, just as one would expect church leaders to discern the pathology of religion in society.

This book concerns such matters and is mainly written as an introductory guidebook for insiders. So, I have assumed that the readership is not especially au fait with the histories and nuances of secularization theories. I am also assuming that the reader belongs to a faith (probably Christian) and, while not knowing much about secularization, nonetheless has some sense of experiencing it and wanting to come to terms with this. Perhaps a bit like a patient with an irritating condition they can't quite put their finger on. Is it age, or possibly something to see the doctor about, or chat with a pharmacist … or just ignore and hope it goes away?

If you have that condition, reading this may help you understand the affliction and what could be done about it, if anything at all. In setting out a diagnosis and prognosis, I do not presume to know what kind of faith the reader might have in themselves or the body of belief they belong to and its current state of well-being. Hence, this guide is offered as a kind of introduction to the field and study of secularization for people who have concerns about faith in public life, society and contemporary culture, and its fitness for the future. So, my working assumption is that you think the issues secularization raises for faith today might matter.

The Exiled Church: Reckoning with Secular Culture is positioned to help reflection in this arena. In using the term 'reckoning', I naturally infer that we must assess, measure, evaluate and examine the state of churches in twenty-first-century life. Few would consider this an easy era in which the churches can expect prompt returns for their investment in mission and ministry. Our English word 'reckoning' comes from a much older fourteenth-century Dutch term, *rekening*, meaning 'to settle or provide an account' (a balance sheet, a narrative, a bill of charges, etc.). The proverbial Day of Reckoning is effectively an audit that assesses profit and loss, debt and credit.

As for exile, it broadly infers deportation, expulsion, migration, displacement, scattering and diaspora. One does not need to spend much time with breaking news to know that those who might regard themselves as exiles – estranged from their homeland – may well be given quite different labels by other nations and communities, in whose name politicians will often dub them as 'illegal migrants', and bar them from sanctuary.

The Hebrew and Christian scriptures are punctuated by exiles – economic, existential, forced, social, religious, ethnic, political and military. It is arguably the commonplace default identity of believers in Jewish and early Christian history. Our English word 'exile' therefore draws on Greek roots ('wander, stray, roam about'), Latin ('banishment, drive out, expel') and other ancient terms that remove peoples from their homelands and render them homeless.

Although we are primarily concerned with the impact of secularization on the churches here, the book also suggests that, like a proper biblical exile, churches are mainly responsible for their displacement in the present day. The consequences of their actions and inaction from the nineteenth century onwards have led to self-secularization. The churches have become more worldly in trying to stay relevant. But in doing so, they have been bound and captive to a self-marginalizing stratagem and have effectively self-exiled. So, they wander, stray and roam, having driven themselves out of public life.

There are multiple ironies to note at this point. Many in the churches think that the way to combat secularization, declining congregations and depleting reservoirs of Christian literacy is to engage in more intensive and extensive discipleship programmes. Many businesses and ministries are built entirely on this premise. Yet the term 'discipleship' does not occur once in the New Testament, though many congregations will have heard dozens of sermons on the concept, as though it were biblical orthodoxy. That points to the scale of religious illiteracy within the churches. Desperate to combat depletion and secularization, church leaders are duped into marketing a solution that sounds plausible and biblical and yet isn't. (Readers can follow this up in the 'what3words?' reflection on pp. 169–78.)

Exile, while not something many would choose, nonetheless functions as a cypher in the scriptures for how God uses the wilderness years to re-educate and purge his people. Exilic experiences – those that the Babylonian Empire inflicted upon the Jews come to mind – were unwelcome to those who were forced to experience such displacement and diminishment. And yet the exile itself, testing though it was, would be the crucible for forging a new faith that learned the lessons from the past and vowed not to repeat the actions that had led to entire generations being displaced and homeless.

So we should be particularly alert in times of exile to those who proffer instantaneous returns to the way things once were or promise short, quick routes across desert paths and wilderness that seem to stretch on for ever. This is where the church is easy prey for quick-fix missional solutions to current deficits or trouble-free answers to vexing moral, social, theological and ecclesial conundrums. When such offers arise, they will have often flirted with or been subsumed into subtle half-heresies.

Let me give one small example: the relatively recent invocation from many bishops for Christians to be more 'Jesus-shaped', and the church to be likewise or 'mission-shaped'. Leaving aside what weight and interpretation to give to the word 'shaped' – indeed not physical, but if spiritual or characterful, then how, exactly? – the apparent problem with becoming a different shape to the one we have is that it assumes a privileged high level of personal agency. In the simplest physical terms, few of us can do much about our height. Our weight, or the lack of it – from obesity to starvation – is often the result of complex social, economic and political factors. Obesity is a disease of the poor, just as starvation is most certainly the same.

Can anyone become any shape they like? In a word, no. Those with the power to alter their appearance will most likely be wealthy, secure and privileged. As Luzia Sutter Rehmann has argued so compellingly in her *Rage in the Belly: Hunger in the New Testament*, hunger, rage and the shape of society are powerfully interconnected in today's world, and more so in the time of Jesus. The dynamics of thirst, starvation, famine, plenty, greed, harvest, drought and social unrest over food shaped the world that Jesus knew.

In the Western world, we largely lack the necessary hermeneutic of hunger to read the Gospels. As we mostly do not know hunger ourselves, we forget how much of Jesus' life revolves around his hunger and thirst and that of others, especially the poor. A hermeneutic of exile and displacement loomed ever present for Jesus' audiences, too. Overall, we choose to settle where we can afford to live and, within reason, eat what we like within our budget. Such luxury was rarely encountered in Jesus' time and was unavailable to most.

Likewise, we simply forget that when John the Baptist ate locusts (Matthew 3.4, which the KJV tells us was 'his meat'), it was almost certainly due to sheer desperation. Locusts usually are only ordinary and plentiful in times of famine. We perhaps forget that following Leviticus 11.20–23, only eight locust types are kosher. The Talmud also informs us that there are over 800 non-kosher species of grasshoppers and locusts. So, for every hundred, only one can be eaten.

Furthermore, as locusts swarm, their entire nutritious clouds would likely be *prohibited* protein sources. So, in mentioning that 'locusts were his meat', we are introduced to a perpetually hungry man in an age of food insecurity, food shortages, regular famines and economic austerity with few remedial measures.

The heresy of assuming we can make ourselves more 'Jesus-shaped' stems from Nestorianism and Pelagianism. The former heresy tended to uncouple Jesus' humanity and divinity. The latter promoted the idea that Christians could contribute to shaping their eternal salvation by exercising moral discipline. But if we live by grace alone, we will be what God makes us.

To aspire to be 'Jesus-shaped' or belong to a church that is more 'mission-shaped' is strangely reminiscent of classical nineteenth-century liberal theologies that went off on searches and pilgrimages to find the authentic 'historical Jesus', only to discover when they found this Jesus, he looked remarkably like the pilgrim-explorers that had gone looking for him. 'Jesus-shaped discipleship' and 'mission-shaped church' are largely fashioned in our image.

It may take a fully established exile before the wisdom and courage is acquired to see this, and in the meantime church leaders will continue to devise more shapes and strategies in the hope that these might arrest the religious recession and spiritual depression.

INTRODUCTION: SYLLABUS

Plenty of opinions exist on secularization in the twenty-first century – the extent to which it might be natural, inevitable, invasive or just a passing phase. I have had an extensive interest in theories of secularization throughout my academic career. It is essential to analyse the performance of churches and all faith communities in the twentieth century. It is necessary to understand what is happening to them, what those inside think is happening to them, and what their differences might tell us.

The Exiled Church presents the issues and ideas raised by secularization using the scaffolding of a typical senior-school curriculum. I have divided the subjects into ten lessons that address topics such as culture, statistics, language, science, politics and the like. There is some half-term reading, too. This is just an organizational framework, of course.

Each lesson is brief – reading the text won't take longer than an ordinary class. Individuals can, therefore, take a lesson a week if they choose. Groups can discuss the lessons over several weeks. Or, if you prefer, pair the lessons with the other materials to make a course covering around six to eight weeks, allowing for the material on assemblies and the different features of the timetable. I have provided some study-guide aids and resources to help with this. They appear at the end of each lesson. I have avoided using footnotes and kept references to a bare minimum to avoid interrupting the text flow, but a guide to further reading in the field is provided at the end.

This 'school curriculum' thematic approach to secularization will allow us to develop a kind of 'conversational pedagogy' – assume a teacher introduces a new subject or topic each week for a discussion and class. The lessons help us think, react and discuss. The lessons aim to be insightful, informative and inquiring to facilitate thinking and understanding. The book does not dictate – that would not be educational – it is rather in the style of a chatty seminar.

Readers will encounter interpretive puzzles in each lesson. Do church statistics consistently point to decline, or is it more subtle than that (Maths)? Why do some regions have better churchgoing rates than others (Geography)? Does the past dictate to the present (History)? Is cultural variety a help or hindrance for churchgoing (Languages)? Does a more technological society automatically mean it becomes less religious (Design and Technology)? Such areas take us halfway.

The second half might seem more familiar subject terrain for some. Does evolutionary theory undermine faith (Science)? Is lack of trust in faith communities and increasing prosperity drawing people away from religious participation (Politics and Economics)? How can we teach faith in a multi-cultural society (Religious Education)? With more time for relaxation and recreation, is religion dwindling in importance (Sport and Leisure)? Should religion be a private matter in contemporary society to enable better civic cohesion (Culture and Moral Education)? There is some discussion about the nature of assemblies, too (the pun is entirely intended), the use of terms and their meaning, and a draft agenda – remember, the school motif is an analogy – on governance and what challenges the institution faces.

Please bear in mind that *The Exiled Church* functions as a guide to secularization and its impact on churches. I have written this for faith-based 'insiders' rather than as a treatise for sociologists. If this curriculum does not cause you to dissent, react, push back, argue further and occasionally agree, then one aim of the lessons will have failed. Like all learning, the best is done through conversation and percolation.

'Percolation' is a critical concept in education, as it acts as a cypher for the gradual distillation of wisdom. 'Secularization', as a term, is relatively modern. Although the word 'secular' has been around for a long time, what we generally consider to be the extensive adoption of the term 'secularization' to describe the decline of religion is essentially a post-war phenomenon.

So, it will take some while to appreciate what is taking place. As with coffee, locality, intensity, patience and aroma are all captured within percolations. No 'instant' solutions can yet be commended (somewhat akin to instant coffee). Because truly granular wisdom takes time to develop and mature within its context. Wisdom percolates. Our experience in the world (society, religion, etc.) is that ideas can take some while to sit, seep, develop and take hold.

Therefore, I have rooted several reflections in Aberdeen, where I live, and Scotland more generally. In so doing, I know from experience the value of drawing on informal conversations, interviews and observations from one specific context and faith communities and their situations. So, I draw on chats, discussions and debates in various contexts to bring together a blended account of the issues and impressions relating to the subject. The subject of secularization is often discussed and taught in the abstract and is prone to be treated as a hypothetical construct. However, I contend that grounded approaches to the subject are the best way of keeping speculative theoretical generalizations in check.

Having one country (6 million population) that we reference in discussions has enormous implications for *all* faith-faring in modernity. In Scotland's public life, the lack of church schools (except for Roman Catholic) and other factors have seen a decline in biblical literacy among the emerging generation. At the same time and somewhat paradoxically, there is (arguably) more sensitivity towards and knowledge of other faiths. However, the overall trajectory points towards religion becoming a private and personal matter, no longer enjoying significant purchase within public life.

I will also draw on examples from Canada, the USA, Australasia and Europe. Furthermore, some of the issues other faith groups face within the UK are also part of the blended picture that emerges in this study. That agenda includes the movement from explicit observance in belief and practices to one where emerging generations of Jewish, Muslim, Hindu and Sikh communities identify with their faith for social and cultural roots but not for day-to-day credence and religious convictions. I do not criticize this trend but merely observe that just as the term 'Christian' can be used very broadly as a culturally distinctive marker, other faith communities also appear to be bound upon the same trajectory.

Although we discuss generational change later in our study, it is enough to note for the moment that all faiths are experiencing difficulties in passing on their beliefs to their progeny. As Callum Brown, Abby Day and other sociologists have noted, this problem began for the Christian churches in the post-war era and accelerated rapidly in the 1960s. For non-Christian faiths, the same pattern is also apparent as third-generation progeny become more mobile, work in professions, and no longer root their day-to-day identity in the religion of their parents or grandparents. For example, younger 'secular Muslims' have now emerged as a substantial demographic across the UK.

The Church of Scotland is steeply declining (40% of clergy will be cut before 2030). True, other Scottish churches (Episcopal, Roman Catholic and Evangelical) are declining less fast, but the demographics of their congregations are hardly encouraging. Then again, the diaspora churches are growing numerically in Scotland. There are also new churches (e.g. Cornerstone Edinburgh and networks of church plants; megachurches such as King's Church). New religious movements are also emerging, notably 'Chrislam', a fusion of Christianity and Islam in Nigeria.

The decline of traditional Scottish Christianity can be evidenced in various ways. The Scottish Parliament does not allow the state Church of Scotland to shape its proceedings. In common with other Western/ developed nations, nationalism, individualism, consumerism and various causes such as climate change and political freedoms act as religious surrogates. In other words, they combine passion and ideology (that then form *values*), which then require different kinds of commitment from those typically expected in religious faith.

Scotland emerges as a representative sample of developed nations, albeit one in an advanced state of secularization. By taking one country's pulse and conducting a deeper faith-health check, we will gain insights into how the rest of the world's faith is faring. In some respects, Scotland functions like a representative shopping basket of goods that assesses the health of any economy.

In some respects, the (Presbyterian) Church of Scotland holds up a mirror to the (Anglican) Church of England. At the risk of framing this in a rather over-elevated way, many Protestant denominations, such as the above, have unwittingly engaged in self-secularization, leading to the ontologizing of organization, bureaucracy and management in churches. Let me unpack that just a little.

Up to the pandemic, the church's response to decline was more and more frenetic investment. A rolling programme of hyperactive mission plans was initiated to arrest the decline and reverse a profound cultural shift. Not one has worked. The Church of England's combat-response strategy was to invest in organizational bureaucracy, intensify congregational identity, and then try to galvanize more support for numerical growth to increase membership. This has resulted in a process of self-secularization – thin models of management and organization poorly understood and badly implemented – leading to spiritual disenchantment, breakdowns in trust and a loss of confidence in the leadership and identity of the church.

The notion of a self-secularizing church borrows from the same playfulness we encounter in *The Last Christian on Earth* by Os Guinness (previously published as *The Gravedigger Files*). Guinness argued that the churches had sown the seeds of their self-destruction, and Christianity had become its gravedigger. The gravedigger analogy frames the thesis that the Christian faith is the single, most vital contributor to the rise of the modern world, yet the church has fallen captive to the very world it helped to create. As the church accommodates the world uncritically, it becomes its own gravedigger. It self-secularizes and has no immunity against its Babylonian cultural captivity brought about by the loss of its integrity, credibility and civility.

Guinness saw the evidence for this in the fads and fashions of modern pragmatic evangelicalism and other traditions. *The Last Christian on Earth* draws on C. S. Lewis' *The Screwtape Letters*. Still, instead of correspondence between a senior and junior devil, Guinness created a fictional dialogue between two council members which aims to undermine the Christian church. The Deputy Director of the Central Security Council gives a subordinate advice on accomplishing their goal. *The*

INTRODUCTION: SYLLABUS

Last Christian on Earth is subtitled *Uncover the Enemy's Plot to Undermine the Church*, which has a touch of John le Carré's espionage novels.

The Deputy Director proposes to undermine the churches through a fivefold penetration, demoralization, subversion, defection and liberation process. Penetration is achieved with some ease; churches hunger for relevance and growth, so are prey to all manner of pragmatic programmes and ideas that might achieve that goal. Demoralization is achieved through the church's hypocrisy and public scandals. Subversion is achieved through church leaders offering mirages of success and strategies claiming a courageous, bold new vision. Defection is achieved when prominent leaders abandon the church to the custody of the gravediggers (who will just keep on digging). Liberation is finally achieved when the church can no longer support itself.

The grave gets ever deeper once the rising ground of secularization, privatization and pluralization are factored in. Secularization and privatization will regard religion as a private matter and as a restrictive force in public life. Pluralization will offer multiple options in material, moral, political and spiritual domains, such that the believer becomes the consumer – choosing the faith that best works for them and, if necessary, tailoring it for bespoke individual consumption. Churches typically respond to the culture of modernity across a push–pull axis. Some cultural trends are resisted and repelled, while others are accepted and actively promoted. Yet, as Guinness notes, churches and faith communities frequently lack the necessary wisdom and discernment to understand the consequences of what they may be uncritically imbibing.

The Last Christian on Earth is artful and playful. Here, I have attempted something similar by playfully drawing on the framework of a school curriculum with its lessons and subjects. However, my intention is entirely serious since churches appear to be unwittingly committed to and engaged in a wide variety of self-secularizing actions that seem to indicate a marked drift away from its fundamental calling and authentic identity. *The Exiled Church* picks up on themes and concerns raised in my books *The Humble Church: Becoming the Body of Christ* and *The Precarious Church: Redeeming the Body of Christ*. *The Exiled Church* will hopefully be followed by the next volume in the same series, *The Pilgrim Church: Returning to the Journey of Faith* (forthcoming, 2027). Unlike *The Humble Church* and *The Precarious Church*, *The Exiled Church* and *The Pilgrim Church* dwell less on scripture and are much more concerned with the currents and crises that are challenging the churches in the twenty-first century.

In this context, *The Exiled Church* explores the position, problems and prospects of faith in public life in the twenty-first century. Any lessons learned will most likely have some critical putative applications for the rest of the world. So, let us begin with the actual terms.

The Very Revd Professor Martyn Percy
Provost Theologian, Hong Kong Sheng Kung Hui; Professor of Religion and Culture, University of Saint Joseph, Macao; Research Professor, Institut für Christkatholische Theologie, Theologische Fakultät, Universität Bern, Switzerland, CH.

Terms of Reference: Secularization

Secularization, a concept of profound complexity and ongoing debate, is often used to describe the recent decline of religion in the Western world. However, this simplistic understanding immediately encounters convolution. For instance, religious affiliation in the USA, a supposedly liberal and modern state, remains robust. On the other hand, Europe is hardly an exception to the general decline in religious interests. Moreover, the relationship between religious interests and factors like industrialization, modernity and globalization is far from straightforward.

Understanding secularization necessitates a historical perspective. It is not a recent phenomenon but has its roots in the past. During the peak of the Industrial Revolution in Victorian Britain, church attendance reached unprecedented levels. This was when new denominations, 'soft religion' and new religious movements were on the rise. The term 'soft religion' refers to forms of personal and collective support that are 'spiritually freighted', such as 'mindfulness', certain types of yoga, therapies and fitness-related practices. While the term 'secularization' has become a standard part of our vocabulary, its true definition is rooted in a cluster of prior sociological understandings.

Defining the Term

Bryan Wilson, one of Britain's most prominent scholars of secularization during the twentieth century, significantly contributed to our understanding of the term. His work argued that secularization is related to the diminution of the social significance of religion, including:

- The gradual sequestration by political powers of the property and facilities of religious agencies, the shift from religious to secular

control of various activities and functions of religion (e.g. schools, healthcare, welfare – BBC TV's *Call the Midwife* tracks this).
- There is a general decline in the proportion of the time, energy and resources that people are prepared to devote to religious concerns (e.g. midweek Bible classes, Sunday shopping, religion fitting around sport and leisure). Post-Covid, the decline is even more marked.
- The overall decay of religious institutions and the supplanting, in matters of behaviour, of religious precepts by demands that are strictly following technical criteria (e.g. codes of conduct at school are unlikely to draw on explicit religious roots).

Other scholars, such as Larry Shiner, outline six characteristics that identify the process of secularization.

1 *Decline*: previously accepted symbols, doctrines and institutions lose prestige and influence. The culmination of secularization would ultimately be a religionless society.
2 *Conformity*: the religious group or the religiously informed society turns its attention from the supernatural to the secular. The culmination of secularization would be a society absorbed in the pragmatic tasks of the present and religious groups indistinguishable from the rest of society.
3 *Disengagement*: society separates itself from the religious understanding that has previously informed it to constitute an autonomous reality and consequently limits religion to the sphere of private life.
4 *Transposition*: organizations, knowledge, powers, authority, behaviour patterns and institutional arrangements once understood as grounded in divine power are transformed into phenomena of purely human creation and responsibility.
5 *Desacralization*: the world is gradually deprived of its sacred character as humanity and nature become the object of rational-causal explanation and manipulation. The culmination of secularization would be a completely rational world society in which the phenomenon of the supernatural or even of 'mystery' would play no part.
6 *Movement*: from a 'sacred' to a 'secular' society. 'This is a general concept of social change [with] multiple variables through several stages … the culmination of secularization would be a society in which all decisions are based on rational and utilitarian considerations, and there is complete acceptance of change.' (Larry Shiner, 'The Concept of Secularization in Empirical Research')

TERMS OF REFERENCE: SECULARIZATION

Charles John Sommerville also suggested six hallmarks of secularization. The first five are essentially definitions, and the sixth is a clarification. Thus, for Sommerville, secularization can refer to processes of:

1 *Differentiation*, in which the various aspects of society, economic, political, legal and moral, become increasingly specialized and distinct.
2 *Transformation* of individual religious institutions into secular ones. For example, Harvard University moved from a predominantly religious institution to a secular one.
3 *Transferral* of activities from religious to secular institutions, such as a shift in the provision of social services from churches to the government.
4 *Transitioning* mentally, from *ultimate* concerns to *proximate* concerns. For example, moderation of behaviour is due to current consequences rather than being out of concern for divine judgement or eternal reasons.
5 *Declining*, with broad patterns of societal decay in all levels of religiosity.
6 *Variability*, some Christian denominations and movements have declined faster than others. Some seem to buck the trend, though the decline impacts all churches. Furthermore, some faiths experience secularization more severely (e.g. Christianity in the USA does, but other faiths and religions are far less affected at present).

We could distil these twelve hallmarks above into just two primary meanings:

1 *Partial, Gradual and Ongoing*, the differential and separation between religion and state.
2 *Complete*, religion (and God) removed from the public sphere, so society becomes entirely functional.

Humanity has few examples of complete secularization. Even when a state acts to remove religion entirely (e.g. certain kinds of communist regimes), the state and its leadership develop a cult-like status. The forms of religion simply morph into worshipping, and faith pledged in the secularity of the state and/or its leadership, as though a deity.

Several objections can be raised against the secularization thesis. First, apparent religious decline (formal attendance at a place of worship or belonging to a religious organization) must be measured against other voluntary organizations or associations. Granted, fewer people formally belong to a Christian denomination compared to the inter-war or Victorian periods. But almost all forms of association have declined steeply since those days. There are fewer Scouts and Guides in Britain, or organizations like Covenanters and the Boy's Brigade. Trade union membership has waned, and there are now fewer members of political parties. Then again, recreationally, fewer people are in our cinemas and football grounds than 70 years ago. Yet no one can say these activities are in decline.

Second, there is reason to doubt that fewer people are turning to official or mainstream religion. For example, the Victorian period saw a sporadic revival of religion and a religious attendance 'bump' that lasted less than 50 years. Yet the beginning of the eighteenth and nineteenth centuries was the very opposite of this: church attendance was, overall, derisory. The evidence for church attendance during medieval times is contestable, with some scholars asserting that religious observance was vital and others arguing that it was, at best, patchy.

Third, this haphazard, semi-secular, quiet (but occasionally rowdy and irreverent) English Christianity continues well into successive centuries. James Woodforde's *Diary of a Country Parson* provides an invaluable window into the life of the clergy and the state of English Christianity in the eighteenth century. Again, a close reading of the text suggests that whatever secularization is, it is not a product of the Industrial Revolution. Woodforde thought it was reasonably good to have 'two rails' (or 30 communicants) at Christmas or Easter from 360 parishioners. Such figures would be low by today's standards in some rural communities. Woodforde tells us that the only time his church is ever full is when a member of the royal family is ill or when there is a war.

Fourth, statistical surveys continually support the thesis that Europe is where most of the population continues to affirm their belief in God but then proceeds to do little about it. So, church attendance figures tend to remain stubbornly low. Yet this is not a modern malaise but is instead a typical feature of Western societies down the ages. Granted, there have been periods of revival when church attendance has peaked. But the fundamental and innate disposition is one of believing without belonging; of relating to the church and valuing its presence and beliefs – yet without necessarily sharing them. Or, as the classic aphorism puts it, 'I cannot consider myself to be a pillar of the church, for I never go. But I am a buttress – insofar as I support it from the outside.'

Scholars are divided on how to interpret contemporary society and its apparent secularity. Sociologists such as Peter Berger have effectively repented of their predictions of the 1960s and now argue that Western society, with all its capitalism and consumerism, remains religious. Historians can now show that increased church attendance may be a response to social unease and dislocation. The Industrial Revolution and the re-settlement of post-war Britain both saw a rise in church attendance that may be viewed as a reaction to social upheaval.

Other scholars, such as Callum Brown and Steve Bruce, have argued that secularization is neither a product of the Industrial Revolution nor of Enlightenment thinking but is, in fact, a relatively more recent phenomenon. Brown argued that the cultural revolution of the 1960s has broken the cycle of intergenerational renewal essential to Christianity's survival. The rise of popular culture has done more than any other thing to marginalize Christianity (and religious observance in general) and provide people with other arenas for absorption and entertainment.

Similarly, Robert Putnam shows that the rise of popular culture in the USA has deleteriously affected many different types of associations and voluntary societies. Putnam's thesis demonstrates that 'negative social capital' has built up so much that religious affiliation may ultimately be affected. In a country where churchgoing is a regular activity – as many as 50% of the population regularly attend, though this is also now declining – Putnam's thesis may point to some interesting future trends.

Danièle Hervieu-Leger suggests that religious memory persists in societies acquiring religious amnesia. Although the invasiveness of popular culture may distort the cycle of intergenerational renewal, her works suggest that religion only mutates under such conditions. It may be pushed from the public sphere to the private realm, but it still appears to be able to shape society at critical points. Far from turning their backs on religion, modern societies seem to be perpetually absorbed by it – something David Martin argued in the last quarter of the twentieth century. More recently, estimable scholars such as Grace Davie, Abby Day and Linda Woodhead have made similar arguments in relation to religious institutions losing ground in public life, while spirituality remains resilient – or can even be seen to be growing fast.

But if this sounds too complacent, it is essential to remember that there is *something* in secularization. True, whatever that process is supposed to describe, it can probably never do justice to the intrinsically inchoate nature of religious belief that characterized the Western European landscape and its peoples long before the Enlightenment, let alone the Industrial Revolution of the nineteenth century and the cultural revolutions of the twentieth and twenty-first centuries.

Standard secularization theories are often unconvincing because they tend to depend on overestimating the extent and depth of Christendom. They assume a previous world of monochrome religious allegiance, which is now (of course) in tatters. But truthfully, the religious world was much more plural and contested before the twenty-first century dawned.

So, what, exactly, has changed? Despite an understandable reticence to accede too much ground to proponents of secularization theses, it can still be readily acknowledged that the twentieth century was one of the most challenging periods for the churches. Leaving aside its struggles with pluralism, post-colonialism, modernity, postmodernity and wave after wave of cultural change and challenge, the biggest issue the churches have had to face is, ironically, a simple one: choice.

Increased mobility, globalization and consumerism have infected and affected the churches, just as they have touched every other aspect of social life. Duty is dead: the customer is king. It is no surprise, therefore, to discover churches adopting a consumerist mentality, competing with one another for souls and members, or entering the marketplace and trying to convert tired consumers into revitalized Christians.

Thus, fewer regular or frequent churchgoers now attend church twice on Sunday, which was once the usual practice. For most, once is enough. Many who do attend regularly now attend less frequently. Even allowing for holidays and other absences (say, through illness), even the most dedicated churchgoer may only be present in church for 75% of the Sundays in any given year. In truth, it is probably declining to below 66%, and heading inexorably to just above 50%. Many clergy now remark on the decline in attendance at Days of Obligation – significant saints' days or feast days such as the Ascension.

The committed, it seems, are also busy. The response from among the more liturgical churches has been to adapt their practice while preserving the core tradition subtly and quietly. For example, the Epiphany celebration may now occur on the Sunday nearest to 6 January, not the day itself. Several Roman Catholic churches offer Sunday Mass on Saturday evenings, for Sunday to be left as a family day, or for whatever other commitments or consumerist choices that might now fall on the once hallowed day of rest. Other accommodations include Sunday evening Mass, which seemed almost unconscionable a few decades ago. Pragmatism and patterns of work and leisure, however, play their part.

Additionally, we note the rising number of 'new' spiritualities and 'soft religions' (e.g. mindfulness). Their range and volume have increased exponentially in the post-war era. Again, choice (rather than upbringing, location, etc.) is now a significant factor in determining the spiritual allegiances that individuals may develop. Moreover, it is difficult to discern the boundaries between leisure, exercise and spirituality. As the consumerist individual asserts their autonomy and right to choose, clear divisions between religion and spirituality, sacred and secular, and church and society are more problematic to define.

Thus, consumerism and choice simultaneously threaten but also nourish religion and spirituality. Spiritual self-help books, other products, various kinds of yoga and meditative therapies, and an ample range of courses and vacations all suggest that religious affections and allegiances are being transformed rather than eroded in contemporary society.

Secular society seems to be powerless in the face of a curiously stubborn (and growing) social appetite for inchoate religion and nascent spirituality in all its various forms. (For further reference, I have listed some of the writers and thinkers at the end of the book (pp. 187–97), which readers might find helpful in following up on some of the ideas here, bearing in mind that the twenty-first century is already challenging perceptions we held in the late twentieth century.)

While many in Western Europe are turning from being religious assumers to religious consumers, and moving from a culture of religious assumption to religious consumption in which choice and competition in the spiritual marketplace thrive, there may be little cause for alarm. Three reasons come to mind.

First, in most modern societies, there is still a demand for a public, performative and pastoral religion. Furthermore, thousands and thousands of private spiritualities and beliefs flourish in modernity, demonstrating that faith does not wither and die in our culture. Instead, religion morphs, mutates and continues to live on.

Second, shared 'vernacular religion' – such as the celebration of Christmas – reveals societies that know and enjoy their carols, nativity plays and other Christian artefacts that long ago moved beyond the control of the church to become part of the cultural furniture. Religion – whether explicit or implicit – is still in demand, and where it is absent it is often created, or the gap is filled with new forms of spirituality.

Third, faiths can respond to the challenge of an allegedly faithless age with a cautious, measured confidence founded on society, which refuses to abandon religion. Often, the best faith communities can do is recover their poise within their social and cultural situations and continue to offer a ministry and faith to a public that still wants to relate to religion without necessarily belonging to it.

Statistics for church attendance, if just read crudely, can look depressing. However, we should remember that secularization is a sociological and interpretative construct based on selected data. Secularization theories tend not to take 'implicit' or 'folk' religion that seriously, and neither do the theorists pay much attention to the rising interest in spirituality. Equally, the appeal of fundamentalism and new religious movements in the West, to say nothing of the explosive growth in Christianity and Islam in the developing world, is also dismissed.

In truth, crude readings of church attendance or membership figures say very little about a nation's faith. As Grace Davie notes, believing and belonging should not be confused. There is space and demand for religion, faith and spirituality in any secular age. This is important, for it reminds us that religion provides enchantment within modernity.

It is essential to see that sociologists will invariably disagree on whether secularization is occurring. Callum Brown, Steve Bruce and others think this is obvious. Charles Taylor has argued that what we now see is 'subtraction' in relation to religion. The more science and technology advance and the greater the pool of universally accessible knowledge, the more religion depletes in proportion. Others, such as Rodney Stark, Robert Bellah and Peter Berger, argue the opposite. There are habits of the heart and rumours of angels in modernity that point to religion's ongoing effervescence.

The approach taken in this book adopts a 'neo-secularization' lens. On the one hand, it is conceded that people increasingly look outside religion for frames of reference and authority to guide their lives. Birth control and roles ascribed based on gender, sexuality and morality are no longer subject to faith-based monopolization. That trend looks irreversible in the twenty-first century, and religious leaders speaking on public affairs are increasingly marginal. In other words, religion has evolved into an opt-in private matter, offering a buffet menu of options, which consumers can select or deselect, decide on proportion, and essentially have full agency to decide on how they consume and own their faith.

On the other hand, as this trend continues, some expressions of religion that appear more resilient in the twenty-first century, though not necessarily growing numerically, are those rejecting this (broadly) consumerist approach to faith. Expressions of resistance are found in all faiths and manifest in ultra-orthodox forms of fundamentalism and various kinds of separatism. Churches of the diaspora in cities such as London, while not necessarily belonging to this group, mirror some of the features due to their ethnic solidarity.

Christian denominations usually see themselves as either the accommodators of culture or resistors. In terms of any church identity, this can lead to some puzzling contradictions. Evangelicals often narrate themselves as resistors of culture, whereas they are primarily accommodators for the purposes of missional relevance. Cultural resistance will be confined to a handful of moral issues (sexuality, birth control, etc.). But history shows accommodation eventually soaks through the polity (e.g. on divorce and remarriage, attitudes to Roman Catholicism, and reasoning with scripture differently on evolution, race, equality and even slavery).

So, is religion in decline? Is secularization on the increase? It does seem to depend on what you mean by religion, where you are in the world, and what your society and culture look like. What I don't think we can accept, however, is that the sacred and secular spheres are separated. They are irrevocably baked into each other.

As we will see at the end of this book, churches now seem unwittingly engaged in a multiplicity of self-secularizing projects without any demand or encouragement from the wider world. Sometimes, when attending church meetings at a diocesan HQ, I have found it hard not to feel that I've been parachuted into a satire, as though someone was making an ecclesiastical version of BBC TV's *The Office* or *WIA*. The line between taking church seriously and a mockumentary was always thin. I fear the line has now disappeared altogether. Overall, the picture is complex. So, we now turn to our curriculum and specific subjects to see if we can find some clues that might help us read and interpret the world around us.

From the Development Office: Change in the Faith Markets

The Current Recession

The 2022 Church of England statistics show that a significant demographic shift in the ministry has been detected and paints a sobering picture. Out of the 7,600 paid clergy, approximately 500 are not in parish ministry but in diocesan, administration or other posts. The age distribution is equally striking, with 14% under 40, 30% being 40–59, and a staggering 56% over 60. Additionally, there are 2,700 non-stipendiary clergy. These figures indicate that the Church of England is on the brink of witnessing the retirement of almost two-thirds of its clergy in the next decade.

As the workforce of the Church of England depletes, so does the volume of work, particularly in marriages and funerals. The Marriage Act of 1994, which allowed non-religious buildings to be used to conduct marriages, had a profound impact. Initially, the adoption of secular civil ceremonies was slow. Less than a decade ago, the CofE was still responsible for nearly 75% of all religious marriages. However, the Church of England's continued opposition to the remarriage of divorcees (if the previous partner is still alive) until the twenty-first century, despite being permitted by Parliament (1969 Divorce Reform Act), left the church isolated. The eventual relaxation of the policy came too late, leading to a significant decline in the Church of England's role in conducting marriages.

Funerals are also a significant part of the religious recession. In 1974, the sociologist William Pickering observed that registrars and funeral directors asserted that close to 99% of all funerals were conducted by clergy or a minister deputed to perform the service. Pickering, writing seven years later in 1981, estimated that something like 75% of English funerals were conducted by the CofE. The clergy funeral workload was estimated to be around 30 per year for nearly three-quarters of clergy – in other words, once every nine days. Ronald Presto, the Samuel Ferguson Professor of Pastoral Theology at Manchester University, concurred with these statistics.

Fifty years later, the figures look very different for the Church of England. The figure for 2024 (estimated) is probably just under 100,000, representing around 20% of all deaths. As a percentage of funerals, the UK has entered an era where the majority of funerals (60%) are now non-religious or are religiously unaffiliated, with 40% of ceremonies being religious. For CofE clergy, that equates to fewer than ten funerals annually if NSMs are included – or one every 35 days.

There are several contributing factors to this collapse. First, the CofE lost its monopoly over consecrated ground for burial. As churchyards and graveyards have closed, civic cemeteries and crematoria have grown, and the CofE is now competing for its market share of funerals on a (er, level) burial ground.

Second, cremations have increased, and the movement of the deceased directly from the hospital to the crematorium, cutting out the home and the local church, cuts out the clergy. Most people die in a hospital, hospice or care home. Death in the home is now very rare.

Third, the last 50 years have seen a steady decline in the clergy's professional standing, their authority in public life, and public trust in the church and clergy. Against this, funeral directors are far more skilled, creative and flexible in their engagement with the bereaved and the dying. They are no longer there to simply convey the body from the church to the ground or crematorium with a slow, dignified journey.

Fourth, the decline in demand for traditional funerals has seen a rise in the personalization of rites that mark the end of life. Bespoke music choices, humour, no sermon, but tributes, poetry and not Bible readings, modes of dress (e.g. the family request you wear bright colours) and celebrating life rather than marking a death are all contributory.

The churches could reasonably argue that they can only accommodate these trends in contemporary culture to a very modest degree without compromising their fundamental identity and integrity. I do have some sympathy with that position. However, the trend towards non-religious funerals seems to be inexorable. In 2022, London CofE clergy took around 4.5% of the funerals for the capital. Nationally, a 2015 YouGov poll found only 25% of the English population wanted a religious service at all to be conducted by a minister for their funeral. However, nearly the same number again did not mind if some religious or spiritual materials were woven into the service.

A Stuttering Religious Recovery?

Faced with these challenges, many denominations have looked at apparent stories of success with a mixture of hunger and envy. Mike Pilavachi's *Soul Survivor* initiative and, before it, Chris Brain's *Nine-O'clock Service* in Sheffield seemed to have a magic formula – a religious alchemy? – for attracting vast numbers of youth. Avaricious glances have also been cast towards Hillsong, an Australian megachurch founded in 1983 that is now a global phenomenon. It has branches in most international cities and award-winning worship bands that tour the world. Their music is sung weekly by an estimated 50 million people in 60 languages. Moreover, the megachurch and its bands have an immense presence on social media with millions of followers, influencing fashion, food and other consumables.

Hillsong's style of Pentecostalism relies on a deep engagement with consumer capitalism, as well as celebrity, youth and digital cultures. For example, many pastors have also become social media 'influencers', with followers then copying tastes in fashion, food, music, art, media, social trends and socio-political causes. Hillsong has embraced movements such as Black Lives Matter, LGBTQ+ advocacy, #MeToo, ecological causes and other campaigns. The scandals around sex and money that have rocked Hillsong in recent times have been reported globally in the mainstream secular media, reflecting the megachurch's prominence. The scandals seem to have done little to dent its spiritual market share.

As with all market trends, it usually pays dividends to look deeper. All that glitters is not gold, and all that grows fast does not necessarily last long. Many of the (apparently) booming evangelical congregations struggle to keep hold of young and middle-aged unmarried professional women who have deserted churches in droves. The same church also cannot seem to have sensible discussions about sexual issues, probably does not have a role for a single successful young career woman and insists on honouring complementarianism and other ideologies of discriminatory belief as having equal integrity.

Younger mothers, likewise, will struggle to pass on their faith to their children. Many will not want to. Some churches are not cut out to be safe spaces affirming generous incorporation. If the churches treat those in civil partnerships, un-marrieds, divorcees and single young women as problems to be wary of or avoid, do the maths. The church will only appeal to around 15% of the population, shepherding a perpetually dwindling flock.

One of the great misconceptions in the post-war era – or perhaps it was a marketing deception? – has been the notion that only evangelicalism or conservative brands of faith could woo young people. But like all such marketing ploys, it had a purpose. It has been an attempt to persuade people who inhabit the wings (catholic or evangelical) that the *true church* and *genuine faith* are only to be found in the more intense, sectarian expression that they represent. And that the middle ground – where the population resides – is starved of 'real' faith and now needs to be evangelized or catechized. Indeed, secularization and the failure of evangelization or catechization are often (still) blamed on the liberal centre ground.

In the meantime, even in the twenty-first century, religion and society continue to be challenged by the Myth of the Popular Right. The myth has a familiar ring to it. The narrative in the post-war era goes something like this: young people like high energy, stimulating worship, clear teaching, strong and stable beliefs, intense fellowship and reliable moral and political conservatism to act as anchors in a world of ideological turbulence and to be swept along by the currents of liberalism and ethical fluidity.

However, recent research in the UK has revealed that many Christian university students affirm their faith in private and stay away from church on Sundays. A Durham University-led study of religion among undergraduates at 13 different English universities also found that liberal Christians outnumbered evangelical Christians tenfold on campus. Christianity attracts far more students than any other religious tradition, but most of these have begun to detach themselves from the church by the time they reach this formative stage. The UK Arts and Humanities Research Council and the Economic and Social Research Council funded the work as part of their 'Religion and Society' programme.

Christianity and the University Experience: Understanding Student Faith, by Mathew Guest et al., surveyed 4,500 undergraduate students and conducted 100 interviews. The research team found that most Christian students were typically moderate in their religious beliefs, tolerant towards others, and liberal in their morality. The study found that very few appear unreservedly supportive of the authority of the churches. The researchers found that Christian students were 'far closer to the social mainstream than the evangelical groups that often speak the loudest among Christians in public debates' and that 'moderate or liberal Christianity is assumed to be a long-spent force once favoured by older generations'.

They conclude that with most Christian students affirming a moderate expression of values in keeping with broader British culture, the church faces a difficult decision about whether to adapt to changing times or risk permanently alienating an entire generation. Furthermore, as educated, upwardly mobile individuals – the future leaders of society – churches risk alienating an important demographic group who could be crucial standard-bearers of Christian tradition.

A Modern Heresy

Secularization is a modern Christian heresy and is believed and promoted by the churches with some degree of fervour. Like most heresies, it looks almost too good to be true, and temptingly so – but is ultimately misleading and doctrinally deviant. What the secularization thesis does is tempt the churches into a dangerous delusion – that God and society are separate, as are the sacred and profane and the church and world. The allure of the heresy appears to give some account for why the churches are depleting and the power and influence of Christianity waning. The secularization heresy then purports to protect the remnants of faith and defend all that is godly and sacred from all that is worldly and profane.

But Christians are committed to the doctrine of the incarnation. Jesus was born into a world of powers, authorities, customs, practices, cultures and histories from which he was not separated. In becoming human and one of us, he then finds faith in the 'secular' world around him, outside Jewish territories, and in people and places that know nothing of Judaism, let alone Christianity. As such, Jesus, in his life, work and ministry, not only bridges the perceived tribal and ideological boundaries of the secular and sacred realms but sets about dissolving them at every opportunity. The Holy Spirit continues that work. Christians now find God in the secular. The secular is not some rival agency that threatens to overrun religion. On the contrary, the secular is now precisely the place where Christians are expected to encounter the work of the Holy Spirit.

This may all sound too much for some Christians because the church has groomed believers into thinking that they possess the truth, and that the world knows nothing of God. Again, we must reckon with what the first Christians understood by faith. We moderns think of it as belief, meaning a set of dry doctrinal and rational propositions. But the Greek word for 'faith' (*pistis*) in the New Testament is better rendered as 'trust in' or 'divine persuasion', rather than 'believe' or 'belief'. Thus, John 3.6 is better read as 'for God so loved the world that he gave his one and only Son, that whoever trusts in him shall not perish but have eternal life'.

I don't have to believe everything a bishop tells me. Sometimes, even as a teacher of the faith, they can just be wrong. Sometimes, with a thin grasp of affairs, their analysis can be weak and awry. Sometimes their media training leads them to say things that are meant to sound good, reassuring and convincing, but they are not true or convicting. I can live with that, in small doses, because belief is not ultimately crucial to our relationships, including those between ourselves and God, and ultimate salvation.

But trust is indispensable, integral and essential to faith. Like doubting Thomas, I may not easily be persuaded, but I am nonetheless asked to trust. I may see the risen Jesus and not know what, how or why I have seen him, and I cannot explain it. But like the women at the tomb, I am asked to trust.

Trust is the key to faith, and it is the key to salvation. When you cannot trust church leaders, no amount of assertion of what is meant to be believed to attain salvation or keep the show on the road will ever compensate for the absence of trust. Faith deserts us at this point. Because if the church cannot be trusted, then nothing it says or does can really be believed.

Children will eventually learn that not everything their parents told them was believable. Spoiler alerts are coming. Father Christmas and the tooth fairy are not true. Sometimes, a parent may tell a child something that, though untrue, was only to protect them from harm or trauma. However, what any child cannot easily recover from is a parent they cannot trust. Faith is trusting in the person, even though you may not have the reasons to believe them (just yet), or the knowledge to confirm your gut instincts and intellectual hunch.

When the church puts its PR or propositional belief statements above trust, it binds itself to a self-secularizing future that only ends in heresy, failure and divorce. True religion is ultimately only secured in authentic trust and love. Belief and knowledge come in some distance behind, in joint third place. Yet church leaders may imagine that if only they keep loudly spouting beliefs and propositions, the tide of secularization will somehow turn. It won't. The Christian faith will continue to recede in public life until trust in church leaders is widely restored. That is, trust to be good, truthful, just, authentic, act with integrity, and be unafraid of scrutiny and transparency. There can be no trust until this is addressed. And that means faith will continue to decline.

The Market – Slowing or Growing?

Secularization is a process whereby increasing and successive sectors of society and culture are freed from the decisive influence of religious ideas and institutions. In other words, this is a movement of change that takes place through the structures of society, especially the spheres of science, technology, bureaucracy and the media, which results in religious ideas becoming less meaningful and religious institutions becoming more marginal. But ... and it is a 'but' ... many sociologists of religion thought faith would be almost dead and buried by now. Peter Berger said as much in 1968 when he claimed that, by the twenty-first century, religious believers were only likely to be found in small sects, huddled together to resist global secular culture.

He had changed his mind some 30 years later. He gave an interview in 1997 and conceded that few now talked of the long night of religion and accepted that what most sociologists of religion wrote in the 1960s about secularization was a mistake. He explained that the underlying theory was that secularization and modernity went hand in hand. However, as the millennium approached, Berger acknowledged that the world was not secular and remained religious.

It is the self-secularizing churches that promote the secularization heresy. It appeals to church leaders as a thesis because it presumes that there was once a golden religious era and that external forces such as industrialization, urbanization and consumerism have caused the decline. Thus, with the decline attributed to external forces and factors, church leaders immediately distance themselves from responsibility and blame. But this won't do as a paradigm. In Britain, only 12% of the population went to church in 1800. In 1850, after a rapid and intense period of industrialization and urbanization, the figure rose to 17%, and remained stable until 1900.

Scottish Methodists may represent the writing on the wall. There may now be less than 150,000 Methodists in Great Britain and Ireland (counted in 2020, pre-Covid-19 pandemic), down from the 617,018 recorded in 1970. Despite an illustrious history of revivalist intensity in the nation dating from 1750 with Wesley's visits, the decline is stark in Scotland. Today, Methodism in Scotland is spread across 38 congregations. The total numbers for Scottish Methodists now amount to less than 1,000.

Meanwhile, the Church of Scotland confirmed in 2023 the permanent closure of seven sites in Elgin, Lossiemouth and across Moray. One of the churches impacted is the historic twelfth-century Birnie Kirk near

Pluscarden, and, once believed to be the oldest in-use church building in the whole of Scotland, has already held its last service. Wooden churches have existed in Birnie since around AD 700 and Pictish stones depicting carvings of fish and birds remain standing in the graveyard today. Birnie Kirk had been holding services for almost 900 years and could justly claim to be older than Glasgow Cathedral and St Giles' Cathedral in Edinburgh. But Birnie Kirk is now on the market and scheduled to be 'disposed of' by summer 2027. The number of weekly congregants at Birnie had dwindled to around 20, with services alternating between there and Pluscarden (which now also faces closure).

That said, social historians and sociologists such as Hugh McLeod have shown that church attendance has been in decline for around 250 years. The 1960s probably represents the era when the decline became most marked and noticeable, with McLeod comparing this 'rupture' to the trauma of the Reformation. However, it wasn't an intellectual thesis, political ideology or theological argument that had caused the decline and rapid depletion of Christianity. It was simply the recognition that there was no obligation to attend church, no means of coercion in belief, as people could now simply *choose* the faith they wanted – or none, if they so desired.

Furthermore, with religious belief and practice becoming matters of opt-in choices rather than awkward social opt-outs, there was now little sense in which faith and religious affiliation functioned as a religious glue. Sunday school attendance declined. Weekends became filled with leisure activities and recreation. Parents no longer taught their children how to pray. Schools gradually moved away from assemblies with Bible readings and hymns. The young were no longer being socialized into Christianity.

Summary

Like its monetarist or consumer counterparts, the spiritual marketplace is subject to various factors, including growth, inflation, stagnation, recession, success, market shares, branding, customer loyalty, investment, consumer confidence, competition, mergers and monopolies. There can be little doubt that the twenty-first century has a vast variety of options – spiritual and religious offerings to suit every taste. But where does this leave the concept of secularization?

A 'hardcore' secularization thesis outlook (e.g. Bryan Wilson, Callum Brown, Steve Bruce) will tend to adopt the decline and conformity positions summarized above. However, most sociologists in the twenty-first century argue for a more nuanced outlook. They urge caution in imposing a sociological theory on complex and contested historical data. For example, it is true that ecclesiastical and political power used to be closer or even joined at the hip. But it does not follow that faith was stronger, more widely accepted and believed in such times.

Historical carefulness and attention to detail suggest that every age has engaged with and accepted religious beliefs and practices in a manner that is subtle and sophisticated. We should beware of trying to make the facts fit the theory. The religious marketplace is complex, and those who imagine they can predict and prescribe long-term consumer trends will usually be proved wrong. That has certainly been the case for churches for at least two centuries and more. However, it is now apparent that the proponents of secularization theories also misread the market trends in the post-war era and have misunderstood the changing complexion of consumer demands and choices.

Ultimately, the spiritual market remains unpredictable – sometimes buoyant, at other times flat. It mixes intensity and extensity, recession and growth, trusted brands with entirely new offerings, and long-term investment with short-term transitional opportunities. As a marketplace, all we can say of the present is that the numbers of spiritual traders, investors, consumers, spenders and savers in the twenty-first century don't point towards an emerging world that is religionless in character, or indeed any society that has ceased to make space for the spiritual. That said, the spiritual market faces other challenges, and we now turn to these.

Opening Assembly:
Inclusive and Impartial

It is a pity that the term 'inclusive' has become very bound up with progressive or even liberal causes. The word 'include' began its life in a different home. Drawing from the Latin phrase *includere*, it meant 'to shut in, enclose or imprison' – just as 'exclude' meant to 'shut out'.

For the record, I don't think the Christian faith is about shutting in or shutting out anybody. Jesus does not especially model or advocate either option in the Gospels. Indeed, by following the pattern of Jesus' ministry, we discover that the hallmark of the Kingdom of God was about something else. Namely, from the Latin *incorporare* – incorporation meant to 'unite into one body'. The incarnation is essentially the action and embodiment of seamless, indivisible incorporation.

It is sorely tempting for faith communities ministering in the public domain to slip into forms of soft inclusion or hard exclusion. Often, these two poles will slug out a war of words on the best pattern to adopt. This might be relativism versus absolutism, conservative versus liberal or traditional versus progressive. These polarized positions will all claim biblical warrant and Jesus as an exemplar.

They are all correct. Jesus was indeed conservative, liberal, progressive and traditional. He was also known to be exclusivist towards some people while being openly inclusivist towards others. Others, preaching absolutism, thought Jesus lacked discernment and standards, and was vapidly accommodating of people who really ought to have been excluded.

Strange though this may sound, there is no *via media* or Golden Mean here. However, churches like to be nice to all and so often fall into the trap of adopting neutrality and impartiality or spend decades trying to 'discern' a way forward in the hope of reconciling the polarities.

This rarely happens, so the church makes concessions to the interested parties, and compromises. In so doing, it hopes to reduce the gap between the polarities, but that inevitably implies that the principles at stake can be diluted or somehow 'salami sliced'. The result of this attempt at inclusivity is alienation and deeper exclusion.

To be fair, churches, like many institutions associated with religion, are also trying to keep some place in the public's affection and sense of ownership. Here again, the temptation is to incline more towards impartial and inclusive outlooks. We see this very clearly in school assemblies, interfaith commemorations and gatherings that have religious aspects but do not necessarily privilege Christianity.

While some faith leaders have assumed this would make religion more palatable in the public sphere of a secularized society, secularism and secularization are not neutral or impartial foundations on which common ground can be established. Many faith leaders have come to realize that any approach that seeks to be inclusive will exclude others. Furthermore, religious, moral or political neutrality and impartiality are positions that must be taken up. They are not the default options arising from a secular society that has found equitable common ground for all. Social unity is not to be confused with social uniformity.

We can all buy into the importance and value of impartial, fair, neutral, unbiased and balanced assessments. We expect our systems of justice to provide nothing less. No one wants to be on trial in a court riddled with prejudice, bias and conflicts of interest. We expect our broadcasters to inform us. We do not watch the news to be groomed into thinking or acting in a particular way.

Institutions and individuals carry the duties and cargoes of social and moral responsibility. However, even before comprehending the values and behaviours we carry on behalf of society for human flourishing, we have to start with a simple, basic, self-critical epiphany. It is this: it is never possible to be non-judgemental. That is why law courts exist, journalists record and report what they believe to be significant (excluding the peripheral), and churches are not communities with any business or vocation to always be balanced.

Counsellors recognize that, whenever they are engaged in therapy, each nod, facial expression, attention to this word, incident or experience, or dwelling on this or that encounter is, per se, a judgement call. Any claim to be non-judgemental lacks existential realization. We simply cannot function as humans without our inner maps and filters. They conduct our affairs of the heart, our rational processing, and our day-to-day decisions. These are complex, social, shared, personal, quirky, wise, irrational, feeling and unfeeling. Humans judge. They are partial. We may strive for balance and harmony, but that decision is bound to be based on our perceptions and, yes, some bias. How could it not be so?

For this reason, I hold that institutions acting in the public interest must be open-minded, but not neutral or impartial. The very nature of public interest requires education and information, contributing to forming individuals and communities in citizenship and fostering collective social and moral responsibility.

We usually regard impartiality as not favouring one position or person over another and being free of bias. Likewise, we associate partiality with favouritism, bias or even one-sidedness. To be fair-minded in each contest is to be even-handed, and we expect this from any referee or adjudication. To be biased is to be more inclined to one side than another.

Balance is usually considered fair, equal and proportionate, such that one proposition or person does not outweigh or dominate the others. The very scales of justice are meant to reflect this. Neutrality is overrated. To be neutral is to take neither side in a dispute, be involved in a conflict that needs to be resolved, or even set some direction. 'Neutral' can also mean literally to be disengaged (e.g. an idle vehicle, motionless).

Public institutions exist to perpetuate moral, civic and social public values down the ages, entirely independent of their actual popularity at any given time. The Church of England, as with any national church, also deals in public religious values. We expect these institutions to be propositional but also open-minded. They must also aspire to be proactive, reactive, steady and stable, yet evolve. They commit to being diagnostic, prognostic and analytical in what they represent, as well as carrying what we might term 'soft values' (i.e. behavioural, dispositional, etc.), which in turn will govern the inner-implicit conduct of that institution.

Without truth, you cannot trust, and without trust, you cannot have any shared reality, society or democracy. The existential threats to our civilization are found in lies laced with anger and hate. In our uberpowered, super-speed world of information technology, we must face the fact that lies, half-truths, rumours and spin spread faster than any pandemic.

Social media drives increasingly narcissistic campaigns, characterized by a lack of kindness, empathy, compassion and consequences. Narcissism others everyone, then dehumanizes them and finally destroys them. We cannot afford to place such a high premium on impartiality that it is blind to facts and truths.

Yet implementing impartiality in day-to-day practice is more complicated than it might initially appear. Most developed nations can bear painful testimony to moral debates driven more by tone than content and more by emotive reactions than reason. The debates on abortion in

Ireland, gun control in the USA, Brexit in the UK and sexuality in the Church of England all come to mind.

With the cultural elevation of 'my truth' or 'alternative facts', the quality of debate and the very reasons for it inevitably suffer. A state of 'truth decay' is around us and within us. Populism can quickly decompose into polarization, atomization and eventual segregation. A defence or recovery of impartiality is essential, but it can never be enough. Christian social ethics, at even the most basic level, teaches that truth can set us free. We need our social institutions to be fundamentally rooted in the truths and values that they contribute to society.

Institutions that put their reputations before truth, accountability, justice and transparency risk eroding the trust that should be vested in them. Perhaps more worryingly, trust itself, part of our shared stock of social capital, decays and depletes. Some competing convictions should never be set within a construction or facade of some faux-balanced debate.

Sometimes, neutrality is simply not responsible. Within such a framework, impartiality is worthy if it implies objectivity, truthfulness, communication and education. This is why respectful, informed debate and analysis are the bedrock for all our great public institutions, whether Parliament or the BBC.

Inclusivity and impartiality are not the answers to the internal problems the church experiences, any more than exclusivity and absolutism might be. In the public domain, there is some evidence that the agency of the secularization thesis has tamed and domesticated religion and pushed it towards both poles.

Inclusivity is seen as tepid and weak, and exclusivity is bordering on extremism and fundamentalism. Unconsciously, churches have colluded with this, making it harder for church leaders to articulate principles within the public sphere. Self-secularization inevitably sets in when churches prioritize their popularity and reputation over their core principles.

Yet, as many have discovered in school assemblies, religious education and other forms of belief, it is better to be honest and clear about the principles of a faith. People will make their minds up about what to believe and practise. There is not much appetite for a confected fudge of neutrality and impartiality. Stick to promoting the core principles. Even a society soaked through with secularization needs these.

Lesson One: Maths

Many churches are already actively serving their communities in essential and practical ways, but how are they serving the spiritual needs of the wider community? To be germane to people's daily lives, especially for those at the margins of faith or beyond, the churches must do much more than cater to different tastes in music. The language of sin and guilt is unfashionable and seen by many as damaging. It's time for us to adapt, to find new ways to connect with our community, to be a beacon of hope and understanding in a world that often feels disconnected. In a culture that wants to dwell more on positives than negatives, the church is grasping for ways to connect.

Let's face the facts. The maths and statistics of churchgoing in twenty-first-century Britain make for grim reading. There are 12,500 parishes in the Church of England. Even before the pandemic, only 33 of these recorded more than 100 under 16s attending church on a Sunday. That equates to a mere 0.26% of the parishes or less than one church per Anglican diocese (of which there are 42). These numbers should serve as a wake-up call for churches.

Most of those churches were evangelical or charismatic evangelical, yet statistics consistently show that these churches also struggle to retain their youth attendance. This is a pressing issue that we must address. Comparing adult numbers across Church of England churches reveals pockets of evangelical intensity (numerical) but not much growth in extensity. Churches must find new ways to engage and retain their youth, ensuring they continue their spiritual journey.

The Numbers Don't Add Up

In conversation with Aberdeen's Roman Catholic bishop, he noted that their main Sunday morning Mass has around 500–600 attending. The Sunday afternoon Mass for the Polish accounts for another 250+. The early 8 a.m. Mass and Saturday evening Mass deliver another 300 attendees. Down the road, the Anglican cathedral records around 120 attendees on a Sunday. Of that, 35+ children attend Sunday school. Around two-thirds of the congregation are Nigerian.

In the same city, the biggest evangelical church is Trinity Presbyterian, but it is not a part of the Church of Scotland. Sunday attendance is around 250. Around 100+ of that congregation return in the evening for praise and prayer. Postgraduates and faculty from the University Divinity School attend in numbers and testify to a good Sunday school for the children, good fellowship for adults, and lengthy, intelligent (but quite conservative) sermons. The postgraduates and faculty don't necessarily subscribe to the theology offered (e.g. no women elders). Still, they opt to stick with the congregation because of the quality of fellowship and teaching. So, there is some dissonance.

The statistics for the Church of England tell a similar story about dissonance. Underneath the large numbers attending evangelical churches, there are real lives that don't and won't subscribe to what the pastor's position might be. This parallels the research into university Christian Unions. Whatever the numbers claimed, many attendees choose to ignore or dissent from the positions taken on gender, sexuality and other faiths.

One Anglican bishop in southern England noted:

> In this diocese, there are six large congregations with hundreds of worshippers, and that also average around over 100 children on a Sunday. Thereafter, we have 120 churches that average around 120 attendees each Sunday (adults and children combined), [another] 120 that have more than 50 per Sunday (total), and then 300+ village churches that will have an attendance of 15–25 on a Sunday, but over 50 at Christmas, Easter and the like.
>
> The conservative evangelical and charismatic evangelical churches collectively give us a figure of 1,500 adults and 750 children. The mid-range churches' numbers (generally not evangelical) amount to 7,500 adults and 3,000 children. The villages, though small, can muster 2,500 adults and perhaps around 100 children between them. Adding that up gives the large evangelical churches some 2,250 attendees and

the rest 13,100. However, overall, only 1.5% of adults attend our churches in [this] diocese, and 0.25% of children. Put together with the notable attrition rate in evangelical churches, no branch of the church can honestly claim it is performing well. (From private correspondence, anonymized and adapted.)

The bishop's perspective reflects the national statistics. The 2022 statistics showed that Anglican attendance at Sunday and midweek services across the UK averaged 654,000, drawn from the population as a whole. The media took their usual potshot, with *The Guardian* noting that there were now more naturists in England than Anglican Easter communicants. The trend towards decline seems inexorable.

Furthermore, there is no sign that any current 'popular flavour' of Christianity is performing better with the wider public than others. Various 'brands' – conservative versus liberal, traditional versus progressive, and so on – may compete for attendees between themselves. However, the statistics suggest that this is more like an internal business-to-business marketing rivalry than a serious sign of notable traction in the public sphere.

While Aberdeen's range of faith communities might provide a rich span of churches and faiths to draw on for this work, to what extent is it representative? Newer diaspora churches originating from Africa form a significant portion of Christian denominations alongside those of established, traditional and historic heritage. There is a wide range of Islamic, Hindu and Buddhist congregations meeting. Aberdeen has Bahai and Jewish communities as well as Unitarian, Mormon and Jehovah's Witness congregations. In addition, Confucian, Theosophical and other institutions that focus on spirituality are also represented. Yet, at the same time, the city also highlights the marked decline in fortunes for the Church of Scotland.

Less than half a century ago the Church of Scotland could claim that it enjoyed just under 1 million adherents out of a population of 5 million. A membership of 920,000 in 1982 had become 270,300 in 2022: a decline of some 70%. The average age of its congregants is now 62 and rising rapidly. It is estimated that only 60,000 Scots worship in person at a Church of Scotland parish on any given Sunday.

In 1982, the Scottish Roman Catholic Church conducted close to 5,000 marriages and could boast that it had 273 men training to be priests. In 2022 there were just 812 Catholic marriages, and 12 seminarians in training. In 2023, the Roman Catholic Church of Scotland attracted just two new seminarians, and it no longer trains priests in

Scotland at all. It may surprise some readers that there ever was, until recently, a Scottish Pontifical College in the heart of Rome (much like the English College). It has now been sold.

The figures for Scottish Episcopalians are not so very different. While the decline is more gradual, it must be reckoned that there were fewer members to start with. In the Diocese of Aberdeen and Orkney, there are 40 parishes (or 'charges'), of which in 2023 one dozen stood vacant. Only one church claimed more than 200 'belonged', though St Andrew's Cathedral and one other could claim 175+. The Communicants' Rolls (those formally registered as members) typically record figures that are 30% less than the actual number of attendees.

In 2023, the number of Episcopalians claiming affiliation to their denomination in the diocese stood at 2,419, equating to around 60 people per parish. Attendances, however, are another story. The Episcopal Church audits the Sunday Next Before Advent for its statistics. In 2023, that Sunday delivered a turnout of 792 persons.

The 2022 census for Scotland produced few surprises. The population is ageing, but still growing. However, what might concern most readers is that the census shows that, for the first time, a majority of people in Scotland say they are not religious. In the 2022 census, 51.1% of respondents said they had 'no religion', which was up from 36.7% in 2011. This dramatic recorded change has been driven by a sharp decline in the number of people describing themselves as being Church of Scotland or Roman Catholic. While the number of Muslims and adherents to other faiths has increased, the movement towards a more secular society continues with unrelenting momentum. The English and the Welsh are not far behind this statistical curve – a decline that leads only downwards. (See https://www.scotlandscensus.gov.uk/2022-results/scotland-s-census-2022-rounded-population-estimates/ and https://www.bbc.com/news/articles/czddpoj488qo.)

Weddings give us a snapshot of what is happening to religion. Indeed, bookings for wedding photographers show that church venues form less of a backdrop for pictures of the happy day. Today, non-religious marriage ceremonies far exceed religious ones in Scotland. Of the 30,000 marriages recorded in Scotland in 2023, only 8,000 were religious. Over 9,000 were Humanist, and the remainder were civil ceremonies. The organizational flexibility of civil ceremonies and the legalization of same-sex weddings has also contributed to largely putting the church out of business when it comes to marriages. Scottish historian and sociologist Callum Brown confirms that Scotland has gone through a profound socio-cultural shift from the last quarter of the twentieth to the first quarter of the twenty-first century. It is now developing into a very secular country.

Downsizing

The data we have sketched so far suggest Scotland's two largest Christian churches – the Church of Scotland (Presbyterian) and the Roman Catholic Church – are now in terminal decline. This presents another difficult maths test – pay and pensions for clergy and the upkeep of expensive buildings. Where does the money come from if the membership is declining and attendance is in freefall? In 2022, the Church of Scotland tasked presbyteries with creating a five-year plan to ensure they were fit for the twenty-first century. The result of such a process is now felt in communities across the entire country.

Churches, including some iconic ancient buildings, are being sold, parishes are being made to merge, posts are being cut and desirable manses are being put on the housing market as the church looks to cut costs and balance the books.

In Elgin, St Gerardine's Church had already held its last service by the end of 2023 and is also to be 'disposed of'. It is now proposed that all the Elgin congregations will combine into becoming one parish using one church: St Columba's South, on Moss Street. To be fair, the central organization of the Church of Scotland recognizes that sacred buildings both possess and add meaning and value to their local communities. At the same time, it recognizes that reducing the number of buildings the church owns is now necessary, no matter how difficult this is.

Yet this rankles local communities. With changing population patterns, markedly different social attitudes and outlooks, and falling church membership, far fewer people training for ministry and a reduction in financial contributions, churches cannot make the maths work. There appears to be no alternative to reducing the number of buildings the Church of Scotland owns.

The trend is undeniable. Scotland is witnessing the rapid depletion of organized religion, nationwide. The decline accelerated in the 1960s and 1970s, fuelled by increasing opportunity and equality for women in the workplace, greater prosperity and more disposable income, and the rapid expansion of leisure activities. Put this together with major shifts in public attitudes to same-sex rights, abortion, contraception and the death penalty, and the social and religious reformation – some may say revolution – is hardly surprising.

This is affecting all denominations across Scotland. Congregations are dwindling, weekly financial contributions have plunged, and many clergy are reaching retirement age. The Church of Scotland's property page currently advertises one of its most prominent churches in Inverness, the Old High Church, for offers over £150,000. Others on the market include churches in Ballachulish (near Glencoe), Orkney, Shetland, Edinburgh and St Columba's, which was Glasgow's last Gaelic church.

Too many buildings with little use are taxing on resources and energy. They need two types of TLC: Tender, Loving Care, yet also Time, Labour and Cash. Churches in Scotland, much like the rest of the UK, find themselves pressured and pushed by their denominational executive management to consolidate, merge and rationalize. Much of the justification for this is accompanied by thin top-down-led apologetics on vision, repurposed mission, growth, effectiveness and discipleship.

Local congregations are sceptical, much in the same way that a scattered and defeated retreating army might be if they were told that their withdrawal and depleting resources were merely a prelude to some great victory. I suppose it is possible, and local congregations live in constant states of hope. But they are increasingly tempered by realism.

As if the implosion within Scottish churches is not enough, the wider environment has become more resistant to religion. Up until recently, Scottish councils were required by law to provide up to three seats on their education committees to unelected religious representatives who would vote on policy and practice. But increasingly, councils are voting to remove them.

Is this an anti-religious trend? I doubt it, and suspect it is driven more by concerns for the expertise and experience of representatives than their faith. Boards of education require high levels of knowledge about the school sector, law, governance and policy from their representatives. Bluntly, most denominations would struggle to nominate representatives who would match their criteria and speak for the church at the same time, just as those denominations would struggle with hospital, adoption, fostering and other boards.

LESSON ONE: MATHS

What Counts?

However, as this is the Maths lesson, please bear in mind the following advice from Einstein before we move on to Geography. Allow me to paraphrase. Not everything that counts can be counted, and not everything that can be counted, counts. The familiar phrase 'the maths doesn't lie' is untrue. Everything depends on what you count, who does the counting, and what *value* is attached to a number. The answer will then acquire a meaning for ends. Sometimes it pays to be sceptical about statistics and surveys.

This is a complex field for statisticians, polling organizations and academics. But if you are part of a faith community and trying to take the temperature, so to speak, which numbers are to be trusted, and why? For starters, and historically, denominations and other faith groups have tended to collect their own data, such as the number of baptisms, funerals, weddings and ordinations in any year. Yet these numbers tell us little about the rates of attrition. For example, how many people who have been ordained in the Church of England no longer practise their ministry within it, and why? There is no real research on these numbers, though they will be significant.

Equally, what numbers are not being counted? I recall a Church of England diocese claiming that it no longer collected or published figures for Confirmations, as these were 'the wrong numbers to be guided by', preferring instead to talk about the number of new congregations, 'fresh expressions' and other enterprises it could promote. When asked how many of these new initiatives were net contributors to the diocesan budget after five years of their existence no actual number was forthcoming. (It was zero, by the way.)

There are faith-based organizations that collect data too, but these tend to be in the service of bolstering a particular position or cause within their respective tradition. In other words, self-confirming, with the thesis directing the facts. So the surest way to get to grips with the maths of secularization is to engage with the academic studies. Here are five brief reflections by way of summing up.

First, even churches that count 'members' lack precision in counting their numbers. If the state of the religious economy is such that many still believe in God, but belonging to a faith-based congregation is in decline, then we may be dealing with a slightly different shift. Namely, believers altering their terms of affiliation to their chosen faith.

Second, the fringes of congregations, even small ones, tend to be thick with people who are very occasional attendees, those who still relate and support but no longer attend, or have other reasons to regard themselves as insiders, when statistics will count them as outsiders.

Third, the quality of religious literacy inside and outside the churches is plainly in steep decline. With the theological education of clergy also subject to fiscal salami-slicing, rationalization, marginalization and other challenges, it is hard to see the road back from here.

Fourth, the churches and other faith groups have endured a collapse in their moral reputations. The public have lost confidence in denominations and faiths due to scandals of sexual abuse, positions taken on sexuality and gender, and increasingly on governance, accountability and transparency. Religious organizations are notably reluctant to commit to external scrutiny or proper independent regulation. The result is an unstemmed haemorrhaging of trust, confidence and support.

Fifth, the secular media, as a consequence of the above, are reluctant to carry yet more news of faiths in decline, mired in scandal, that are unrealistic, disingenuous and even dishonest about what is required. The media remains interested in religious news but is rightly averse to senior religious leaders trying to use press, radio and TV as a vehicle for their own ends.

While it is true that some evangelical charismatic, diaspora and Pentecostal churches have recorded growth, and their congregations tend to be larger, there are far fewer of them. These congregations represent consolidated forms of religious intensity, which explains their attraction and numerical size. However, despite their laudable outreach, such churches lack widespread *extensity*. Cities, market towns, urban and suburban environments will be havens for such congregations. Rural contexts, less so.

For discussion

- What stories do the maths in your congregation and denomination tell you about secularization, believing, belonging and religious affiliation? Do you think there are other ways of reading your maths, or should other figures and statistics be considered?
- Do the figures you have discussed point towards issues, challenges and futures that you can address now, in the present?
- Lieven Boeve states:

    ... secularization emerged as the direct consequence of functional differentiation ... diverse sub-systems emancipated themselves from the all-embracing religious horizon ... [religion] lost its prominent role, [the] all-encompassing source and point of reference for human values and convictions ... religion was forced to take on the form of a subsystem, developing, among other things, its own logic, institutions and role patterns. Religion came to focus exclusively on the promotion of the religious function in society, side by side with, yet distinct from, the other institutions. In doing so, religion was forced to withdraw from public life, its relevance reduced to the organization of the private arena and intimate relationships, side by side with the fulfilment of a comfort/consolation function. (*Interrupting Tradition*, p. 39)

Do you agree with Boeve?

Lesson Two: Geography

Geography and history are hardly strangers to each other, and, as we shall be sketching in the next two lessons, everything is connected. We will be looking at Britain, Ireland, Italy, Scotland, Australia and America to explain how the interwovenness of these places both shapes and is shaped by religion and the lands in which faith settles. This can only be a sketch, but if we want to gain an understanding of when, where, why and how secularization impacts religion, we need some account of how faith arose in any particular context.

It will be obvious to readers that the tense history between India and Pakistan, and disputes over borders, terrain and geography, are religious in origin. Likewise, in many cities across the developed world, religion plays a part in the zoning and populating of an area. Sinister examples include the enforcement of Jewish ghettos. But we can also point to a modern city like Shanghai, still with a notable French quarter. Or Catholicism in Macau arising from its Portuguese establishment.

Twenty-first-century Maps

The dividing lines separating societies and nations and splitting communities are different in the twenty-first century from those at the turn of the twentieth century. Borders, wherever they are, constitute places of exchange between parties and serve as demarcations for identity. Here, religious geography is an inherently complex field. Anglicans, Baptists, Methodists and other faith groups don't tend to select the areas and houses they live in based on their denominational identity.

Yet other religious groups have done so. House churches, Brethren and other newer denominations provide many examples of effectively trying to colonize a cul-de-sac or a particular street. This is more obviously noticed in relation to other faiths in the UK over the last 50 years, with neighbourhoods, districts and sometimes whole towns becoming Muslim, Sikh or Hindu.

Historically, due to the systemic economic and political oppression of Roman Catholics well into the nineteenth century, many British cities contained areas of housing that were shaped by Catholic identity. The rivalry between Protestants and Roman Catholics lives in the football clubs of such cities. There are Church of England parishes where a significant percentage of the population is drawn from one Caribbean country or just one region of Africa.

Any consideration of religious geography in Scotland would have to take account of the waves of immigration, periods of occupation, conquests, famines, forced migration and more. When considering how religion functions in any land, one must understand its social, political, ecological and geographic histories. Geography does not survey the static.

Nations and communities are evolving constantly, and the would-be geographer, much like an ethnographer or anthropologist, needs time on the ground to understand the larger frames of reference that might be appropriate to describe peoples or places.

New alloys of belief can be beguiling. For example, left-wing individualism (which can be doctrine in almost any mainstream political party in the developed world) presumes that all people need is opportunity, a level playing field, education and a bit of graft. True, equality should give everyone an equal chance. But it is more complex than that. Factors like wealth, class, social spheres, strata, poverty and opportunity still determine people's lives in the twenty-first century.

As a rule, denominations, congregations and dioceses are not very good at recognizing their visible and invisible classist assumptions. This is strange when one considers how chapel and church distinctions in the recent past often pivoted on class as much as belief. Or, for that matter, how early Pentecostal churches and their distinctiveness were earthed in class and ethnicity, not just on emphases on religious experience.

Mapping Class and Culture

Writing a century ago, H. Richard Niebuhr was keenly aware of how elite Episcopalians in the USA were in contrast to poorer inner-city congregations and denominations. Niebuhr thought that the effort to distinguish churches primarily by referencing their doctrine and approaching the problem of church unity from a purely theological point of view was fruitless, so he turned from theology to history, sociology and ethics for a more satisfactory account of denominational differences. His study of the social character of the Christian churches was intended to be a practical contribution to the ethical problem of denominationalism.

Niebuhr (like Max Weber before him) linked Protestant denominations to the growth of capitalism. Niebuhr saw that many forms of Protestantism embraced the development of capitalism and moved to individualistic rather than collective concerns. He was particularly insightful in his discussion of how denominations dealt with the issues of slavery and secession from the Union in the American Civil War (1861–65). The churches that had begun as 'movements of the dispossessed' with an emphasis on the equality of God's children would have been expected to condemn slavery.

But in the Confederate South, no mainstream denomination condemned slavery – it was regarded as an economic necessity. Christian native tribes in the war mostly fought for the Confederates, as the taking of slaves – whether from other tribes or captured Europeans – was commonly done. All denominations divided in the war, with the Northern churches continuing to condemn slavery (and slave owners) and the Southern churches proclaiming the importance of slavery to protect an 'inferior' race. Only when war ended did the denominations patch up their differences – or not, as in the case of Southern Baptists and Confederate Methodists.

The first British ships arriving to colonize Australia in the wake of Captain Cook's 'discovery' carried soldiers, convicts, chaplains, explorers, scientists and others. On board Cook's first wave were 12 Jewish people but no Methodist settlers. Methodists convicted of a felony were disfellowshipped, so a Methodist convict was an oxymoron. The same was not true for Roman Catholics, who were over-represented in the penal colonies. Anglicans would be the presumed default denomination for anyone not declaring an alternative allegiance.

On Cook's first voyage, encounters with indigenous groups resulted in some hostilities, but for the most part the meetings were marked by curiosity, wariness and hospitality. Cook's first voyage was scientific, collecting plants, animals and data – especially mapping the stars, oceans, land and reefs.

Some indigenous people saw this as an opportunity to collect samples too – from the explorers. One member of Cook's crew got so drunk one night while on watch he had failed to wake up, let alone raise the alarm when some natives climbed aboard the vessel and removed his ear lobes as trophies.

The early Australian settlements relied on forms of social ordering, discipline and reform that derived their authority and rationales from either military or religious sources. Rather like New Zealand, much later, cities developed social and denominational characteristics that were more apparent than any counterpart left behind in Great Britain – though Belfast, Liverpool, Glasgow and parts of London provided essential indicators of how social and class divisions were rooted in religious identity.

In Australia, Roman Catholicism has historically been the religion of the poor, convicts and labourers. Anglicans and other Protestants, in contrast, have generally enjoyed higher social status and far greater wealth. Just as the end of the Great War saw renewed tensions in Ireland, civil war and then cession, the faint ripples of such divisions are replicated in Sydney. It is not possible to understand the DNA of Sydney Anglicans without having some grasp of modern Irish history, as the tribal Catholic versus Protestant rivalry is rooted in the distinctive cultures that were exported to Australia from the eighteenth century onwards.

Divisions Survive

Even today, the legacy of inter-denominational rivalry lives on, regardless of its roots. Most twenty-first-century folk in the developed world will regard religion as a private matter, and faith as something discreet. They do so despite the evidence of conflicts in Northern Ireland, Bosnia and Rwanda, and presume these to be rarities. However, religious divisions in communities that weaken the collective identity and economics of a city or country are commonplace.

For example, almost every major Scottish town and city was once divided between Protestants and Catholics. Even a fairly small city like Dundee hosts two football teams, with two football grounds virtually next door to each other.

In Edinburgh, the Hearts–Hibernian derby is another Protestant–Catholic rivalry. Rangers and Celtic (Glasgow), likewise, reflect sectarian division. Class plays a part in all of this, too. Notably, Aberdeen remains the largest city in Scotland with only one football team – a direct consequence of its negligible Irish-Catholic population. Our point here is that, economically, Scottish football is weakened by the legacy of its religious sectarianism. Due to size and other factors, only Glasgow, Edinburgh and Aberdeen can sustain their football. Dundee is only fractionally smaller than Aberdeen, but divides its football loyalties, economics and support due to old and long-forgotten sectarian divisions.

Denominations have *evolved*. The major mainstream denominations in Australia have a history of enjoying enormous social influence in an emerging country with few formal social structures. However, in some respects, their evolutionary story of the last 250 years is one of slow secularization, marginalization, fragmentation and disintegration. There is an apparent domino effect.

The Anglican Church still clings to its original monarchical entitlement – especially to speak on social and public matters – and presumes that the wider population will be receptive. But just as Irish Catholicism has struggled with successive scandals on forced adoptions, paedophile clergy, the covering up of sexual abuse, and opposition to same-sex unions, divorce and remarriage, so has Australian Anglicanism.

This has been of the same order, via its historic involvement in education, welfare, the treatment of single mothers, fostering and adoption; yet also differently in respect of the treatment of indigenous peoples and other groups. As such, Australian Anglicanism inherited and incubated similar problematic behaviour patterns that also have some commonality with Canadian Anglicanism.

Geography and scale play a part in this colonization. In lands where the distances between settlements are simply vast, the long arm of the law could be thousands of miles away from addressing abuse of any kind. Religiously motivated social control can be highly oppressive and extremely abusive. Only recently, in an age of affordable travel, fast social networking and communication, did the history of these abuses emerge.

The Protestant–Catholic religious divisions in today's Sydney, however, go some considerable way to explaining the spiritual DNA of its distinctive brand of Anglicanism. However, it is not possible to gain a more comprehensive grasp of the dynamics at work in Sydney Anglicanism until the early history of the Plymouth (or 'Exclusive') Brethren is engaged. Plymouth Brethren are a low church and non-conformist Christian movement whose history can be traced back to Dublin, Ireland, in the 1820s, and in their separatism from the established Church of Ireland. John Nelson Darby (1800–82) was their founder, but they can also trace their origins to the proto-Pentecostal Catholic preacher Edward Irving and his followers.

The late eighteenth and first half of the nineteenth century were febrile and fevered times, with many fearing the end of the world itself. Raised in the recent wake of the American and French Revolutions, and contemporaneous with the threats of Napoleonic conquest and tyranny, the British upper class and aristocracy were living in fear of their way of life being annihilated, and their lives ended too. It is hardly surprising that 'End-Time' sects emerged.

Plymouth Brethren generally see themselves as a network of like-minded free churches, not as a Christian denomination. They will usually refer to themselves as 'Christian', rather than as Brethren. Their first meeting in England was held in December 1831 in Plymouth, Devon. Their meetings were soon simply referred to as 'Plymouth Brethren', although the term 'Darbyite' was also used, especially when describing the 'Exclusive' to distinguish from the 'Open'.

The movement spread rapidly throughout the United Kingdom. By 1845 the assembly in Plymouth had more than 1,000 people. Overseas missions took place very early on, with the successful establishment of 'meetings' in Switzerland and parts of France. Attempts to plant meetings in Baghdad, Madras and other cities were failures. Darby made trips to the USA and to Australia (the latter as early as 1852), where these missions enjoyed considerable success.

Over the years, the Brethren have suffered schism (between 'Open' and 'Exclusive'), and also struggled with some of the issues familiar to new religious movements. These have centred on money, sex and power, order and control, and also included charismatic leadership. However, to this day, Brethren membership continues to confound sociologists and sceptics, and holds its own across the world.

To some extent, their growth (organic, with negligible external recruitment) turns on the tight compacts formed between locality, separatism, business and faith. For example, Plymouth Brethren in south-west England were prominent in local fishing industries, as they were in Aberdeen. The businesses were small and family-owned, and autonomy was easily maintained. Agriculture and farming businesses in Australia offered the same ideal commercial conditions for sustaining separatist community life, while also guaranteeing income.

While the impact of nineteenth-century evangelical revivals in Scotland faded in the twentieth century, there were spontaneous outbreaks, including Jock Troup's mission among fishermen of the north-east in 1921. We note this here because it produced an unforeseen legacy that persists to the twenty-first century, namely the extraordinary proliferation of ice-cream parlours and confectionary shops in most Scottish coastal towns. As the revivalism spread, so did temperance, and with that the sale and consumption of alcohol declined, as did the number of bars.

But as the Americans later discovered under their own prohibition era, banning alcohol drives up sugar consumption. From the late nineteenth century, Scotland had already seen a steady but modest increase in Italian immigrants after the Republic had been declared. In the aftermath of the First World War, many Italians experienced extreme poverty and famine in their home country, with some walking across Europe to find new work and homes, mainly from the provinces of Lucca and Frosinone. The numbers emigrating to Scotland increased significantly, plying their trade in confectionary and catering.

Summary

Let us return to Sydney and Ulster. The peculiar culture of Sydney Anglicanism has taken more than 175 years to gestate and is the result of tribal intermarriage (almost literally) between various Brethren and Anglican families, and a general if inchoate understanding that the interests and outlooks of these two tribes are near-identical. Both groups are socially and politically conservative, and anti-progressive-liberal.

On some battlefronts, therefore, Sydney Anglicans will join forces with their Roman Catholic counterparts (e.g. on opposing the legalization of same-sex equal marriage). Doctrinally, however, the Brethren-Anglican alliance will decisively reject Roman Catholicism, and vice-versa. These mutual doctrinal denigrations can be quite vehement.

Here again, Sydney has more in common with Glasgow, Liverpool and Belfast than it does with any other modern city in the twenty-first century. Religious divisions run deep and are hard-wired into the DNA of the culture. Unlike their British counterparts, Sydney's divisions have seldom required any kind of close physical proximity to the 'othered' neighbour who is deemed to be following an entirely different faith.

Those who puzzle over how Sydney manages to be multi-faith, multi-cultural, rainbow-tribal and highly diverse – and yet also hosts a version of Anglicanism that has more in common with the Exclusive Brethren than any other expression of Christianity – need only develop a cultural-spatial understanding of the city. It isn't really a city in the way many Europeans use the term. It is more like a series of connected districts, with quite local-tribal loyalties, which in turn have detectable social, political, religious, ethnic and demographic aspects.

Tribally, this brand of Ulster Protestantism is also committed to monarchical patterns of polity, and despite the congregationalist nature of the ecclesiology, churches are in fact subjected to high degrees of centralized control and authority in the hands of an elite. In terms of their overall identity, Sydney Anglicans will narrate themselves and their mission in much the same way as English Protestants did in seventeenth-century Ulster. This is a masculine and muscular mission, and the perceived hostility of the environment that might resist such a gospel only confirms that this ministry is mainly for men. The men expect their will to prevail, and to be obeyed. Sydney Anglicans are settlers in a heathen land, bringing the pure truth and light of the Protestant faith (and rule) to those who dwell in darkness.

For discussion

1 Discuss the geography and landscape of your local faith communities. To what extent does wealth, class, housing, demographics and other factors shape the profile of your congregation?
2 What would a future map of religion in your locality look like?
3 Graham Neville said:

> The average English Christian (which is to say, the average lay person) seems always to have taken an eclectic approach in matters of belief. Perhaps that is due to the historical experience of the English people in the turmoil of the Reformation period. Today, most churchgoing members of the Church of England are lukewarm about apostolic succession, but look for reverence in worship. They reject the notion of a collectivist society, but believe that their life in the secular world is the proper place to work out their discipleship. They accept the need for open-mindedness in interpreting and even criticising the scriptures and formularies of religion, but continue to reverence the Bible and to accept the historic creeds, whatever private reservations they may feel about a faith once delivered to the saints and hence immutable. (*Radical Churchman*, p. 14)

Is there an English attitude to religion? If so, how would you characterize it now, and what do you think it might be evolving to become?

Lesson Three:
History

If aspects of white upper-class idealized Victorian-Edwardian missionary religion were examples of 'muscular Christianity', then the present promotion of such faith is best described as necrotic. The nineteenth-century German pathologist and anthropologist Rudolf Virchow (1821–1902) first coined the term. Virchow noted that as the cells in our bodies die, bone density, the resilience of skin and internal organs all become weaker. The human body becomes susceptible to external injury, infections and disease, and to internal collapse due to the ageing process, along with less and slower blood supply to the tissues and primary organs.

Thus, while the body continues to function well, the ageing process poses ever-higher risks to the anatomy. The pathology is a given. So, even a form of muscular Christianity such as Sydney Anglicanism or, for that matter, other forms of (seemingly) endlessly renewable and ever-youthful faith are subject to necrosis.

Understanding Decline

I realize that Sydney Anglicans would deny such ageing processes, but history is essentially the study of progressive and regressive ageing, and there is little we can do to avoid it. Time only moves forward, and the past and present are always the best indicators of what is most likely to happen next. In *The Great Dechurching*, Jim Davies et al. begin their study with the observation:

> In the United States, we are currently experiencing the largest and fastest religious shift in the history of our country ... for the first time in the eight decades that Gallup has tracked American religious membership, more adults in the United States do not attend church than attend church. This is not a gradual shift; it is a jolting one. (p. 3)

We will be exploring American religion later in this book, but for the moment this is a seminal point in our history lesson and overall syllabus. Historians like to look for the causes of events and trends, so are there any in the USA that might help us understand secularization slightly better? Here are a few suggestions to get us started.

First, religion in the USA has historically been a matter of freedom of choice, and this has created a consumer faith-fest that has endured for more than three centuries. Immigration to the USA was also bolstered by exiled religious groups, either persecuted or surplus to requirement. The history of the nation is, therefore, in debt to significant pockets of religious intensity, who, on arrival, were religiously self-catering or occupied territories where nobody could interfere with their freedom of religious expression. Mormons, Jews, Puritans, Zoroastrians, Amish ... the list is long.

Second, a basic principle of history and economics is that religious competition produces growth. The north-west of England and west of Scotland have a significant history of Irish diaspora, and Protestant–Catholic rivalry is found all over Liverpool, Glasgow and other towns. In Yorkshire, the Irish diaspora was relatively weak. No competition between rival denominations meant, historically, less growth. For hundreds of years, churchgoing rates were significantly greater in Lancashire than Yorkshire.

Third, when the rivalry stops, the growth slows, and the religious economy will reverse after a while. There was religious competition in Yorkshire, of course, namely between non-conformist chapels and the established Church of England. However, once this religious differentiation ceases to be significant – because of changes in social mobility, class, wealth and education – religion ceases to have much value as an identity marker. With competition dwindling, there is a residual beneficial bounce for the one option remaining – but this is just a reprieve for all parties.

Fourth, another factor at work is relative economic prosperity and stability. There was a time when it was hard not to encounter a breathless write-up or book about 'explosive church growth' in South Korea, China and other East Asian countries. The growth was indeed phenomenal. But it has levelled out, steadily and rapidly, in the twenty-first century, impacted by economic growth, alternative leisure activities, technology and more individualistic and therapeutic spiritualities that are more appealing to the emerging generation.

Country Cultures

We'll be looking at Millennials and Gen-Z in the second half of the term, but for the moment it might be helpful to reflect on the perspectives that we carry through the history we have been taught at school. Most readers will presume that the USA is a natural guarantor of religious freedoms, while a country like China is not. Four observations are worth noting here.

First, when we think about a country, it pays to remember that nationhood has often arrived quite late in its people's history. Canada, Switzerland and Italy are obvious examples. The United Kingdom was not formed until 1707, and Ireland was subsequently co-opted in 1801. The USA began with 13 states, and now has 50. China is an alloy of regions, nations and peoples. All these examples have a central government. Each of these examples has wide-ranging regional variables in terms of laws, customs, languages and culture.

Second, it may surprise some readers to know that the Chinese Communist Party *does* guarantee religious freedom. But like in the USA, what counts as 'freedom' and 'religion' are qualified terms. Can you display the Ten Commandments in a courthouse in Tennessee? Legally, the answer is no. This is not secularism at work. Rather, it is a nuanced constitutional understanding of what counts as public space, and how that is to be protected.

Third, and likewise, what private beliefs can a citizen hold and express in the privacy of their own home, and air in public? It would be hard to find any country where personal beliefs expressed in private space are illegal unless they are criminal. Equally, it is hard to find any country where free rein is given to any citizen to express any opinion, religious, political or otherwise, in public space or publish it.

Fourth, while it may seem self-evident to many Westerners what 'religion' and 'freedom' must mean, we would do well to remember that these are qualified terms with histories and will mean different things in Muslim nations, too. Furthermore, even in one country, there will be significant regional variations. Some religious views aired publicly in one US state may earn applause and accolades. However, the same sentiments uttered in different states might land the speaker in serious trouble for breaching the peace, with the police and lawmakers getting involved. Generally, it pays not to generalize.

Fifth, the public and private nature of religion figures differently in societies according to inculturation. To take the Anglican (Episcopal) Church in Taiwan, for example, there are no objections to women priests by the church or on theological grounds. However, the wider culture is very resistant to women priests (so there are lots of women deacons), despite Taiwan being a Province of the American Episcopalian Church following the Japanese surrender to the USA in the Second World War. Furthermore, in sharp contrast to Hong Kong and Macao, Taiwan does not permit religion to be taught or preached in schools, and maintains a sharp distinction between public and private, civic and personal. Religion is regarded as a private, personal matter.

Faith Down Under

To return to the Australian history of secularization, Irish Protestant identity can now be seen to account for Sydney Anglicanism's rapid rise and eventual fall. The history of secularization in Australia accounts for the blending of Sydney Anglicanism and its anti-Catholicism and the same social conservatism that is resistant to same-sex unions. It explains tribalism and its elitist and classist aspects.

In their time, Irish Protestants were the wealthy minority and at home in the upper echelons of the British class system. Thus, charming, mannered, fiscally secure, public school (boarding) educated, and with powerful ingrained attitudes to gender – the right kind of masculinity (muscular, cerebral, anti-emotional) is prized. As is the right place for women (submissive, pliable and rooted to their assigned roles in the home). This is all accompanied by an abhorrent fear and loathing of male same-sex relations. The ascendancy of such religious outlooks is not hard to comprehend, in the same way that their eventual disintegration is also entirely predictable.

The fairest characterization of Sydney Anglicans engaging with other Provinces in Australia and the wider Anglican Communion is deliberate *disassociation* from the Anglican tradition, coupled to intensive missionary endeavour. Here, it closely follows the pattern of the Brethren 'meetings' of the mid-Victorian era onwards. Indeed, Sydney Anglicans will use the term 'meeting' interchangeably with 'service'. Many churches in the diocese do not use a prayer book or a liturgical form of service. Few churches sing canticles and responses.

But the striking feature of all church services is the worship – idolizing, essentially – of the Bible. It has a totemic status. It is God-like: it cannot err, is perfect, pure and to be reverenced as though it were ... well, God. Correspondingly, no formal liturgy is used, since it may detract from the worship and adoration of scripture. Some elements of

Anglican liturgy may still be used for congregational participation, such as a corporate confession of sin, the saying of creeds and some corporate prayers.

Lay participation in Sydney churches also occurs through Bible readings, leading intercessory prayer, leading the meetings, testimonies and interviews, singing and playing music. In many parishes, alcoholic communion wine has been replaced with grape juice. Usually, the reason given for this is to be sensitive to people for whom alcohol may cause a problem.

Sydney Anglicanism has more morphological resonance with the Plymouth Brethren (and its Irish sectarian expressions) than any other denomination. If you can close your eyes and imagine an upper-class Australian version of the Revd Ian Paisley (pre-Good Friday Agreement), you will have captured an essential essence of the leadership of the Diocese of Sydney. Their motto, or perhaps mantra, is: 'Wherefore come out from among them, and be ye separate, saith the Lord, and touch not the unclean thing; and I will receive you' (2 Corinthians 6.17, KJV).

As any student of congregational studies, anthropology or ethnography will confirm, generalizations can only be made after extensive and intensive grounded fieldwork. Immersion is key. There are some high-quality anthropological studies of Sydney Anglicanism now beginning to emerge, and here I will simply mention a few of the key observations from those conversations, as well as my own interactions with clergy and laity in the diocese and corroborating my own 'thick' conversations.

First, the local Sydney Anglican congregations are diverse in character and composition. Members of congregations I spoke with personally talked quite freely about pushing the clergy to preach for 8–12 minutes and would regularly or frequently tell their clergy that 20-minute sermons tended to be flabby and repetitive. Clergy I spoke with thought that anything less than 20 minutes was 'merely a homily, and so not proper teaching'.

Second, most of the laity I spoke with thought that subjects such as women and sexuality were not issues that concerned them, but rather something that consumed the minds of the clergy. They spoke longingly for hearing a message that was hope-filled, inspirational, relevant to their actual lives and wise. Despite this, laity spoke appreciatively of their clergy, and expressed affection for them – though clearly not agreement with them.

Third, one anthropological study was intrigued by the mode of pedagogy that was used to teach laity. Sermons – often lasting 30–40 minutes – would frequently be reinforced with PowerPoint illustration, with questions (and the 'correct' answers) flagged in relation to the subject being addressed. Attendees are often given handout sheets for the sermon, comprising headlines, questions to follow up, with blank spaces provided to fill in the answers. The attitude taken to the Bible is that it is a factual manual, and therefore to be learned and applied, as one might take a manual to a car, domestic appliance or heating system.

Fourth, the anthropological reflection on the 'sermon slot' notes how the approach to teaching adults has more in common with Sunday school or kindergarten, with take-home sheets to fill in, and mutually reinforcing patterns of authority, ensuring (literally) that everyone is on the same page. The communal reinforcement of the sermon's message is explicit – 'turn and share with your neighbour what you have just heard'.

Fifth, the attitude to scripture is a form of pseudo-science. Or is perhaps better understood as a specific mode of congregational engineering. The Bible is read as a 'manual', and applied to the breakdowns, repairs and maintenance in the life of a Christian. Thus, if facing the prospect of a divorce (family or friend), you may hear, 'Turn to chapter X and verse Y of Book Z' as the answer and the means of resolution. The Bible is, therefore, akin to some kind of car repair manual.

Sixth, Sydney Anglicans – clergy and laity I spoke with – were decidedly lukewarm to the new 'Province of the Southern Cross', with some openly expressing cynicism and disinterest. Likewise, GAFCON was a subject that meant very little to the people I spoke with, some of whom suggested that this might be an ego trip for the leadership but had nothing to do with the clergy and congregations of the diocese.

Seventh, both clergy and laity I spoke with expressed profound dis-ease at the declining numbers of young people engaged in church life. They were divided, however, on the causes. For example, the largest university church in the city (St Barnabas Broadway) saw the students threaten revolt and secession over the stance of the diocese on same-sex unions. They compelled the Rector to make their views known to the hierarchy, and he (reluctantly?) obliged.

Eighth, recent census data indicate that Millennials and Gen-Z are unpersuaded by the gospel, according to Sydney Anglicanism. This mirrors the current situation of churches in Ireland. The authority of the clergy and church hierarchy has been eroded and rejected due to revelations of abuse and malpractice. Yet the church still presumes to instruct the population on what to vote for and against. The people vote with their feet.

Sydney Anglicanism is sectarian, for sure. But the roots of this stem from antagonisms locked into early Irish Brethren secession and a complex spaghetti of class-related issues. It continues to be shaped by the residual attitudes still found in working-class and middle-class Irish Protestantism, including its Ulster branches with Orange Orders (more formally known as Loyal Orange Institution, and meeting in Orange Halls or Orange Lodges). Yet Sydney Anglicanism is also wealthy, elite and well connected to the upper echelons of Australian society.

This is partly through schooling, with fee-paying single-sex denominational boarding schools still accounting for some of the very best education money can buy. Add the colleges into the mix, and the history of the Church of England in the continent, and you can easily see why Sydney Anglicanism has a permanent seat at the high tables of Australian society. Thus, the polity functions and behaves like a disenfranchised sectarian minority but continues to wield the kind of clout that upper-class Anglicanism can still muster in England.

Finally

Another significant historical example to note in the apparently rapid advance of secularization is the movement of the Anglican position on families in the early twentieth century. The church began to phase out its support of the large family in favour of smaller households and, by extension, supporting the use of contraception in response to the changing needs of its communities and congregants. Recognizing the potential economic benefits and greater social control to be gained by individuals, particularly for women, with the aid of family planning, the church embraced and endorsed it for the greater good of the communities they served.

In addition to historicizing their approach, sociologists of religion look to lay the foundations of their research on experimental or experiential evidence. This approach underpins inference from large-scale narratives with solid, evidence-based conclusions. In this spirit, sociologists examining congregants in the USA have connected class and denominational identity. For example, a 1987 sample of US church membership found that almost 40% of Episcopalians earned over $40,000 per annum, compared to just 14% of Baptists.

An anecdote related by Max Weber supplies a further illustration of the invisible link between class and denomination. A German dentist who had moved to the USA was taken aback when a patient, before disclosing any other, perhaps more pertinent, information such as medical history, informed him of their denomination to convey what they thought he needed to understand of their situation: a concept perhaps alien to a European. The patient wanted to prove their social standing, perhaps their wealth, to their healthcare provider – and in their eyes this was the quickest route to this understanding.

Despite the diversity of offerings for churchgoers and the increased ability of individuals to cast their net as widely as possible in terms of transportation, class-denominational symbolism, unaffected by locale, persists. Across North America, Episcopalians, Presbyterians and Methodists are thought of as the 'upper' denominations of class, and Baptists and Evangelicals are considered 'lower'. This helps to explain the rather snide and classist remark in the opening of Norman Maclean's novella, *A River Runs Through* (1976): 'My father (a Presbyterian minister) always told me that a Methodist was a Baptist that had been taught to read.'

Denominational identity is entwined with ideas of wealth and, by extension, social standing. Additionally, the 'spectrum' of denomination is informed by ethnicity: many Pentecostal and 'Gospel' churches are composed primarily of African American worshippers, while denominations on the Protestant end of the scale see most white congregations.

H. Richard Niebuhr's research examines how these factors shape congregations as a 'practical contribution to the ethical problem of denominationalism'. He perceives the formation of congregations as fundamentally dialectical: disinherited and established, nationalist and sectionalist, immigrant and of 'the colour line'. In interrogating these oppositions, Niebuhr sought to uncover deeper unities between congregations that draw from such distinct political and social identities.

Niebuhr wished to prove that American Christianity crystallized around ecclesial and doctrinal proclivities and the broader social-economic-political forces working within religious and secular communities. Methodists and Baptists, for example, by merging their identity with a 'frontier ethos' in the south and west of the USA, gained more tremendous popularity among potential worshippers than more reserved and established denominations (e.g. Episcopalians and Presbyterians).

To account for the persistence of factors of class and race in shaping North American religious affinity, we can cast an eye over the demographics of the colonies. As David Hackett Fischer argued, the 'regulative culture' of each of the groups that settled early America persisted, for a couple of centuries, coding manners, customs, law, attitudes to class, the economy, liberty, society and individuals.

Thus, East Anglian Puritans settling in what became Massachusetts, Quakers of the north Midlands in Pennsylvania and the Royalists of the Southern Counties, who fled to Virginia during the Civil War, all brought to their fledgling communities their own ideas of how to live, how to be a citizen, how to worship. The strong markers of identity that drove those people to seek out unknown territory in which to freely forge their own unchallenged ways of worship and governance have left their trace in subsequent generations, in both implicit and explicit forms of leadership in both congregations and wider communities.

We can furthermore find more specific illustrations of this in the history of festivity in the 'New World'. The development of new communities afforded the freedom to keep or dispense with traditions. Cromwell's staunchly Puritan England looked to end the celebration of Christmas with the threat of fines, which was replicated in the New World by loyal followers. Puritan celebrations, in keeping with their outlook, were frugal and prudent, and very strict.

Pennsylvanian Quakers went further to distance themselves from frivolity and hedonism, by sweeping clean the calendar of any markers of festivity. Months became numbered instead of named; the Sabbath or Sunday became the 'first day', as 'all days are alike holy in the sight of God'. The Quakers also carried the spirit of their deeply held commitment to social justice in their food preferences, refusing sugar because of its dependence on the slave trade, and salt because of the belief that the salt tax paid for military activity.

In contrast, the decadent, transposed Cavaliers of Virginia were keenly and extravagantly observant of the full Christian calendar: Christmas, Whitsun, Shrovetide, Hocktide and Twelfth Night were richly celebrated with feasts and festivity. Fischer's account paints the picture of a jubilant society that embraced 'parties, dances, visits, gifts and celebrations', and delicacies such as fried chicken and fricassee.

If such large-scale organizers of duration and action, like food and the scheduling of seasons, were subject to such cultural distinctions, it is not hard to imagine granular units of social order such as economy, rank and power and leading worship being subject to the same distinctions. Signifiers of class distinction, such as the position of a seat and the company kept in church, clothing, and conventions in behaviour and manners upheld were as rife in the 'New World' in the sixteenth century as in medieval England; and what's more, were encountered in each denomination – certainly in the settlements named above. Underlying this visible stratification of status through social cues, symbolism and mannerisms were the invisible, implicit theological assumptions that this mirrored a Divine Order – thereby regulating society according to both a worldly and otherworldly logic.

Of course, each of the 'folkways' that Fischer identifies had views on the appropriate place of religion in society and what role religion could play in public space. To a large degree, each of the folkways had their reasons for wanting to keep religion as a private matter with freedom of conscience. Having been evicted from Europe because of their religious views, they had no desire to blur the boundaries in the New World.

For discussion

- Do you think history shows us that a decline in religious observance is inevitable in modern society?
- What lessons from the past suggest that secularization itself is sporadic?
- Raymond Aron said:

At the risk of shocking sociologists, I should be inclined to say that it is their job to render sociological or historical content more intelligible than it was in the experience of those who lived it. All sociology is a reconstruction that aspires to confer intelligibility on human existence, which, like all human existences, are confused and obscure. (*Main Currents in Sociological Thought*, p. 207)

Is Aron right?

Lesson Four:
Languages

What is the third most used language in the USA? English is first, probably Spanish second ... but third? It is not Chinese, Italian or German, although German was once the second most spoken language in the USA until around 1800. The third language in the country is American Sign Language (ASL).

During the Covid-19 lockdowns, many people baked bread or watched Netflix. Others, like 17-year-old Mariella Satow, spent their time changing the world! Mariella has dual citizenship in the USA and the UK. At the start of the pandemic, she happened to be in New York and couldn't leave due to travel restrictions.

As Mariella embarked on her ASL learning journey, she discovered a lack of resources available to her. She thought that seeing an ASL interpreter in action might aid her learning process, but to her surprise she found that movies and TV shows on streaming platforms didn't use ASL interpreters. They may offer closed captioning or audio description but no ASL. This realization ignited a fire in Mariella, a determination to change this fact. This determination led her to create an innovative solution, a solution that is now changing the way the deaf and partially deaf community experiences movies and TV shows.

Mariella's solution to the lack of ASL interpreters in movies and TV shows was to create an app. This app, which uses a simple Google Chrome extension, adds an ASL interpreter to the corner of movies. Its purpose? To allow people who are deaf or partially deaf to watch both the movie and the interpreter simultaneously. Recognizing the importance of accessibility for children, Mariella decided to focus her efforts on the Disney+ platform, a platform she believes children watch the most. But she didn't do it alone. She sought the help of ASL teachers and the deaf community, making them an integral part of the solution.

With hearing impairments in the family, they all learned sign language. Broadcasters and streaming platform companies suggested using subtitles. However, sign language encompasses facial expressions, hand movements, arm gestures and body language. Subtitles and captions lack emotion. They can't convey background noise or emotional literacy. They can't express or show love – only read it out. The development of the SignUp app took about a year. This sleek app is already bringing immense joy to kids and parents.

One parent who praised the new app pointed out that words require actions to be meaningful. There is a limit to what we can take from some captions or text. We often need to know how the words were spoken, in what context and to what effect. Without knowing the emotional tone of a sentence, we may be lost in understanding what feelings are being communicated. Philosophers of language often talk of speech-act theory and perlocutionary effect – *how* we use words to say something that warns, warms, threatens or encourages.

Sign Language

As I have often remarked, Jesus is the 'body language of God' – God's sign language to us. Jesus hears the unheard, sees the unseen, embraces the unfelt and neglected, holds the rejected and speaks for those not spoken for. It is not just what Jesus says, but how he says it, and in what context and to what effect. To be sure, language is complex.

If we are to come to terms with the self-secularization that the churches have embarked upon, language is a fertile field for further enquiry. After all, what's in a word? Perhaps you may recall the UK launch of *The Independent* newspaper in 1986. It was memorable for many reasons. This was the first broadsheet newspaper to be launched in the UK in 112 years. The newspaper founders – dissatisfied with the ding-dong battles between Robert Maxwell and Rupert Murdoch slugging it out in circulation figures, scoops and advertising revenue – sought to establish a newspaper free of mogul ownership.

One of the more striking features of the newspaper was its marketing, with Paul Arden and Tim Mellors leading the team at Saatchi & Saatchi responsible for creating the advertising campaign. Who can forget the giant billboard posters: 'It is. Are you?' Just four words, and then the title of the newspaper. As zeitgeist captions go, they are hard to beat.

Now, you might think you know what 'independent' means. But in the 'church world', where the laws and culture are different from the 'real world', language functions differently. A bit like Alice in Wonderland, in the church world, when leaders use words, they only mean what the leaders say they mean. Take a word like 'independent'. It means 'free from outside control; not depending on another's authority' (e.g., 'the study is independent of central government').

However, this may not be the definition applied by senior church leaders. 'Independent' could mean, 'It wasn't me that did or decided this: it was s/he, her/him, they/them ... but they came to the same conclusion as me, and honestly, I did not influence their decision ... and they are not me, so they are independent.' In other words, 'independent', in episcopal hands, could mean a separate person agreeing with a decision the bishop has already made.

Of course, it is true that a term like 'independent' can be used in a relatively pliable way. My local coffee shop is 'independent', which means it is not a branch of Costa, Starbucks and the like. But my local independent coffee shop has three branches. Next door to the independent coffee shop is the independent bakery – it has seven outlets. OK, it is hardly the national bakery chain Greggs, I grant you. But if the bakery had 40-plus outlets, is this now an 'independent chain'? 'Independent' is a commercially positioned identity. It connotes local and is not owned by some faceless foreign conglomerate. It may even mean it makes pastries rather than buying them in bulk. Fair enough.

So when the Church of England uses the term 'independent' in safeguarding, what does it mean? Is it 'free from outside control and not depending on another's authority' or the more commercially local definition? No. Plainly, it is a PR term and not proximate to genuine independence.

Thus, the Diocesan Safeguarding Advisor (DSA) in your diocese will sometimes be referred to as 'independent'. But they are paid by the diocese, accountable to the Diocesan Board of Finance, work in the diocesan HQ, and are ultimately accountable to their bishop.

When Words Mean Something Else

A few years ago, I wrote to the Archbishops of Canterbury and York to complain that an external appointee had been hired and briefed without a process open to independent scrutiny. The individual appeared not to be acting independently, but in a more partial and protectionist manner on behalf of existing power interests, including church lawyers, senior officials and PR agents. The Archbishops' response to me began: 'We obviously have a different definition of what "independent" means to you.'

They went on to explain that the way they used the term 'independent' had to be *qualified*, and to factor in that, to some extent, they were inevitably controlling the outcome of the 'independent process', and had authority over it, as they were paying for it. But all of this was still 'independent', they maintained – in a way that one might argue the Isle of Wight is unattached to England.

Put like this, then everything in the Church of England is independent of everything else in the Church of England, and that is also sort of true, right? Parishes are independent of each other. Clergy too. Dioceses, when it comes to questions of maternity leave, housing allowances, moving expenses, employment ... are, well, all independent of their neighbouring dioceses. Having your own definition of words can work really well in certain kinds of cultures and kleptocracies (i.e. George Orwell's *1984* or Margaret Atwood's *The Handmaid's Tale*).

The Post-truth Church

Churches used to talk a lot about sin and hell, but hearing a sermon on either topic today would be unusual, and even novel. Most congregations would find it deeply uncomfortable. Unless, of course, it was about other people's sins, with the likelihood of the perpetrators heading for hell in a handcart they have made for themselves.

One of the strange features of contemporary culture is the relatively rapid disappearance of the doctrine of sin. As David Lodge remarks in his novel *How Far Can You Go?*, it seems as though hell disappeared in the 1960s and that nobody noticed. And if there is no hell, then there is no vehicle – such as sin – that can take us there. Hell, therefore, becomes an abstract concept, something to gaze on and ponder in literature and art, perhaps puzzle over in primitive religion, but only to ultimately rejoice in our deliverance from such a manipulative and fear-inducing theological construction of reality.

Now, no one likes to talk about sin; it is guilt-inducing, moralizing and anti-social to do so. Yet we ignore the concept at our peril. We run risks of propagating general, vague morality, yet rooted in little that might offset this. Moral, but no compass, if you like. We know that for the emerging generation, acquisition has replaced aspiration; vocation has given way to fulfilment. People know what they want to have but not what they want to be. Our heroes are no longer persons with exemplary lifestyles; they are individuals who are free to indulge in conspicuous consumption. We are raising a generation who aspire to wealth but not necessarily to goodness.

This brings us, neatly enough, to the problem of sin in modern society. Even the mention of the word seems faintly problematic. Few Christians (let alone others) appreciate churches that dwell on sin and moral shortcomings too much. In our therapeutically attuned culture, the very concept has been somewhat downgraded. Sin may induce guilt and shame. Such concepts, we are frequently assured, are constrictive, paralysing and unhealthy.

I recall a survey conducted many moons ago about children's attitudes to sin. The findings suggested that the concept of sin was becoming rather old-fashioned. Even children from quite religious families struggled to explain what sin was. One child said biting his sister was 'quite bad'; another said that jumping on the sofa was 'naughty'. And from their schools, including Church of England schools, the children seemed to have learnt that the great evils of our time are global warming, pollution and bullying. And the answers to these vices? Take more care of the world, recycle and be nice to others. They're not wrong in these prescriptions.

A culture mainly formed through desire and achievement may find itself in a subtle temptation. Namely, confusing sin with imperfection, what we lack as people, and how to achieve greater fulfilment. Falling short, in other words, but not by much. Yet a society that plays down the idea of serious personal and social sin, and even unfashionable concepts such as original sin, does so at its peril.

In ignoring the dark side of human nature, there is a risk of collapsing into a falsely optimistic and even utopian worldview that struggles to cope with the reality of evil. Rather than accepting sin as commonplace, modern societies often presume to regard a state of sin as exceptional – even as a private matter.

I suspect that one aspect of the problem may lie in language. Sin is a short, simple word – almost too easy and quick to utter. The very accessibility of the word has arguably played a part in the weakening of its power. Our older and arguably denser religious vocabulary preferred the word 'trespass': 'forgive us our trespasses as we forgive those who trespass against us'. The word captures something active: the idea that lines have been crossed, that some of the things we say, do and think are offensive, and that we grieve God. 'Sin' is just one example of a word that has lost its currency in contemporary culture.

Slippery Language

So, if such terms are now out of fashion in the churches, what language is being spoken in them? Increasingly, it is a rather nebulous, elastic corporate-speak.

A simple example will suffice for illustration here. Take the three groups set up in the wake of the decision to approve same-sex blessings. They are the Pastoral Guidance Working Group, the Pastoral Reassurance Working Group, and the Prayers of Love and Faith (PLF) Working Group. All chaired by bishops, their task is to 'to draft outline proposal[s] for the minimum structural provision that is both necessary and proportionate'. The phrase, on its own, looks innocuous enough. But break the sentence down and you get:

- 'minimum structural provision' – decided by whom?
- 'necessary and proportionate' – decided by whom?

These are relative terms. My sense of proportion may be quite different from someone else's, which I could regard as disproportionate. What is 'necessary' – and for what ends? Who is defining 'minimum', 'structural' and 'provision'? The terminology is loaded with potential for good and harm, yet it sounds so inoffensive. The groups are also about 'process' and 'progress'. But some might conclude that the process is all about making sure there is no progress.

In other words, nothing must lead to an outcome that might make some walk away or leave. Such terminology can script a scenario in which both parties dislike one another, rarely speak, and live completely separate lives. Yet both parties refuse to initiate divorce proceedings, afraid of losing reputational face, dividing assets or blinking first. However, despite their long-term separation, they continue to use the same surname and home address. But no one is fooled, and it is hard to have trust and confidence in an institution that appears unable to make clear moral decisions.

Language is important here. How does the oppressed person 'speak' truth to power structures? Who decides who is oppressed? If someone feels oppressed due to their gender or sexuality and is then offered equality, will that really oppose those who have their own theological reasons for perpetuating discrimination?

Language is the issue here. Constructing words that are managerially geared towards a *via-media* outcome is often unintentionally oppressive and discriminatory. Ursula Le Guin distinguishes between 'mother tongue' and 'father tongue' (*Dancing at the Edge of the World*, p. 149). The 'father tongue' is the language of power: 'spoken from above ... it goes one way ... no answer is expected or heard ...' The 'father tongue' is the clinical language of the management meeting – it distances the emotions, passions and desires. It will speak of 'proportionate process' with an unerring fluency.

In contrast, 'mother tongue' is the language of the home. It is, according to Le Guin, 'inaccurate, coarse, limited, trivial, banal ... earthbound, housebound, common speech, plebian, ordinary ...' However, for Le Guin, the 'mother tongue' is also the language of connection and relationships; its power lies in uniting and binding, not dividing. It is Le Guin's contention that much public discourse, especially professional discourse within institutions, is a learned 'father tongue' that deliberately marginalizes the realm of feelings and the scope of relationality. She argues that a recovery of 'mother tongue' within public discourse is essential for the reconstitution of public life, where 'plain' speaking can reclaim its proper value (or currency) as bona fide expression.

It is often the case that in relationships where the expression of anger is denied its place, resentment festers and breeds, and true love is ultimately distorted. Strong feelings need to be acknowledged for relationships to flourish. If strong feelings on one or both sides have to be suppressed for the sake of a relationship, then it is rarely proper to speak of the relationship being mature or healthy.

For example, in cases where sexual or some other abuse of power has taken place (say on gender, sexuality or other 'protected characteristic' in law), the church may seek the compliance of the abused and rarely censure the abuser. It may go further and express the hope that the victim finds healing and peace and gets pastoral care. Gentleness and love that is detached and self-sacrificing have often been held up as the virtues that Christians should be striving for, as though there was some ideal Christ-like civility that the church was striving for.

Now, civility is certainly an important virtue in the church, but often with little acknowledgement that the *form* and *patterning* of polity have normally been established by those in power so that, consciously and unconsciously, their privileges are maintained. At the same time, we may need to appreciate that anger and fury can be correlated with violence and chaos, and their intimate connection with love is not acknowledged. The expression of passionate feelings, or perhaps of any feelings, can be seen as a threat to the polity that maintains the power of an emotionally detached rational faith.

Summary

Learning to listen to narratives that convey solid and powerful feelings and experiences of abuse and marginalization is a significant and costly task for ecclesial polity and pastoral praxis. Ultimately, the anger of those who seek justice may help the church to move on from its 'tamed and domesticated' spirituality of suffering for its own sake and work instead for the abused.

This means listening to the experiences of abuse and marginalization that have led to aggression and anger and seeing them as far as possible from the perspective of those with less power. It means humility on the part of those who hold power and an acknowledgement of the fear of losing power and control. It means a new way of looking at power relationships that takes the gospel seriously. It means churches and leaders getting in touch with our feelings and developing an emotional intelligence that can lead to a new kind of ecclesial intelligence. And this, indeed, is what we want from our leaders. People who can receive and handle feelings – even strong ones – and sometimes communicate the same when necessary.

Under such circumstances, one can begin to conceive of the possibility of 'truth speaking to power (structures)'. For this speech to happen, the institution's power structures and framework must be robust enough and sufficiently humane (i.e. compassionate and empathetic) to understand that a 'theology of reception' requires churches to receive coarse, vernacular and strongly articulated feelings. Moreover, such feelings cannot and should not be silenced or pasteurized as a precondition of receiving pastoral care – and, ultimately, justice. Where care and justice are denied, the church has a prophetic task to foster 'loyal dissent' until it is faithful to its incarnation and vocation – namely, to be the feeling, sensing body of Christ that proclaims the Kingdom of God.

For discussion

- If it is true that people are increasingly sceptical about how religious leaders use language, what is the remedy?
- With trust and confidence in religious leadership falling, and in political discourse 'truth decay' endemic, what can churches do to restore authentic, clear language in our moral, social, religious and political decision-making?

LESSON FOUR: LANGUAGES

- Peter Berger wrote:

  To ask sociological questions, then, presupposes that one is interested in looking some distance beyond the commonly accepted or officially denied goals of human actions. It presupposes a certain awareness that human events have different levels of meaning, some of which are hidden from the consciousness of everyday life ... we will not be far off if we see sociological thought as part of what Nietzsche called 'the art of mistrust'. (*Invitation to Sociology*, p. 41)

  Given that 'the art of mistrust' can be important for healthy institutional life, what spheres and actions within the church should be subject to wariness, qualms and scepticism?

Lesson Five:
Design and Technology

One could be forgiven for thinking that northern Europe continues ever onwards to a more secular existence. However, if you worship in an English Anglican cathedral on a regular basis, this will not be your experience. In this brief and rather eclectic reflection on English religion, society and secularization, I propose to reflect on just some of the reasons why Anglican cathedrals seem to be faring rather well, when other churchgoing is in decline.

It is fair to say that most cathedrals in the Church of England possess their own unique and complex 'ecclesial DNA'. Some began as monasteries, while others as parish churches. Some were purpose-built; but others may no longer reside within the bounds of the original span of the diocese. Some are ancient, some modern. Most are a mixture of the two. David Martin, commenting on English churches more generally, noted:

> We in England live in the chill religious vapours of northern Europe, where moribund religious establishments loom over populations that mostly do not enter churches for active worship even if they entertain inchoate beliefs. Yet these establishments guard and maintain thousands of Houses of God, which are markers of space and time. (David Martin, 'Believing without Belonging', cited in Grace Davie, *Religion in Britain Since 1945*, p. 189)

The recent British Social Attitudes Survey seems to confirm those 'chill religious vapours', as the survey found that whereas 33% of Britons aged over 75 still identify as Anglican, the figure for 18–24-year-olds is just 1%. In the Netherlands, 15% of Roman Catholic churches have been desacralized in the last 25 years, and the figures for Protestant churches are 25% – a quarter of the buildings have now been put to alternative use.

To be sure, it is something of a trope to say that while individuals become less religious, they become more spiritual; or that while belonging declines, believing persists. The sociology of religion continues to propagate such binaries with characteristic suppleness. However, I want to add one more dimension to the debate. Namely, that with every advance that secularization may make, sacralization keeps in step.

Subtle Spirituality

For many English people in the twenty-first century, religious establishments are perceived to have weathered rather badly. Secularization and consumerism, coupled to a declining number of those who follow a faith, and a perceived loss of integrity in religious institutions, has led many to question the future of public religion. However, Martin suggested that the buildings – these very stones – still speak to us:

> Not only are they [i.e. churches] markers and anchors, but also the only repositories of all-embracing meanings pointing beyond the immediate to the ultimate. They are the only institutions that deal in tears and concern themselves with the breaking points of human existence. They provide frames of reference and narratives and signs to live by and offer persistent points of reference. They are repositories of signs about miraculous birth and redemptive sacrifice, shared tables and gift-giving; and they offer moral codes and exemplars for the creation of communal solidarity and the nourishment of virtue. They are places from which to launch initiatives that help sustain the kind of networks found, for example, in the inner city; they welcome schools and regiments and rotary clubs; they are islands of quietness; they are places in which unique gestures occur of blessing, distribution and obeisance; they offer spaces in which solemnly to gather, to sing, to lay flowers, and light candles. They are – in Philip Larkin's phrase – 'serious places on serious earth'. (Martin in Davie, *Religion in Britain Since 1945*, p. 190)

Cathedrals are primary exemplars here: ultimate places of spiritual spatial inclusion. Yet, there is no denying that in the twenty-first century there is general anxiety about apparently declining numbers of attendees at regular Sunday worship in the Church of England. However, at least one group of churches has bucked the trend: the cathedrals.

Consistently, the numbers worshipping in English Anglican cathedrals have been resilient, immune to the decline seen elsewhere. Indeed, many cathedrals report an increase in the number of worshippers. But what do these numbers actually show? As with much statistical analysis, the story behind the numbers tells us how to interpret the bare arithmetic. One needs to grasp the nuanced ecology of English churchgoing to understand the growth of worshippers in cathedrals.

Here, I draw on conversations with David Martin (1929–2019) and am especially mindful of his view – that I share – that Anglicanism, at least in its English form, is a support-based institution rather than a member-based organization. To be sure, one perpetual question that Anglicanism faces today is, 'Who is Anglican?' However, any investment in overly narrow specifications of membership will have profound consequences for the identity and organizational shape of Anglican ecclesiology, including performative-liturgical arenas such as baptism. The socio-cultural expectations invested by those outside the worshipping congregation in baptism require constant local, pastoral negotiation between churches, clergy and the communities they serve.

The socio-theological vision of Anglican polity therefore needs to understand its purpose and roots more deeply. Theology and the supernatural authority of the church, which it is called to embody and proclaim, cannot simply allow its ethos, identity and practice to be replaced with what I have consistently termed 'consecrated pragmatism'. (For my earliest discussion of this, see Martyn Percy, 'Consecrated Pragmatism', *Anvil*, pp. 18–28.) This is particularly the case about how people become part of a social and spiritual body, like the church, that is fundamentally inclusive in nature and character.

Just About Managing

The current turn towards ecclesial organization and management focuses particular attention on how people become part of the church. Specifically, it presses the question as to whether the global expressions of Anglican polity are distinctive, bounded and overtly member-based organizations in character, seeking clarity of identity, or whether they are broader social and sacramental institutions to which a much wider public relates in a variety of ways. I am mindful that most ecclesial ecologies will contain both elements and will be a blend of those who feel a sense of strong attachment (often expressed as 'membership') and those whose basically affirmative relationship to the church involves a more variegated form of commitment.

My concern has always been with the concept of membership in Anglican polity. If the church is consumed with its own managerial and organizational goals, including increasing its own numerical growth and intensifying the commitment of its members, it will have lost its soul. I hold, in contrast, that global Anglican polity posits a rather more incorporative model of church; a non-member-based institution that seeks to serve society, rather than a member-based organization that primarily exists for its committed subscribers.

Churchgoing in Anglican polity has generally been a matter of relating to and inhabiting a complex institution, where the idea of 'membership' of a subscriber-based organization is seen as a more 'Congregationalist' kind of ecclesiology. I mean no disrespect to non-conformist chapels and congregations here. I simply draw attention to the fact that a parish church exists for the spiritual well-being of the whole community, and it serves that community independently of any subscription or support that the people in the community might provide. This is by no means a unique characteristic of Anglicanism.

It is the form of ministry exercised by ecumenical chaplains in prisons, hospitals, schools and colleges, the armed services and other arenas, where the ministers elect to serve the whole body, not merely the committed minority. There are some figures that seem to buck the trend. The numbers attending cathedral worship have, so far, shown some resilience to the long-term religious recession that blights most local churches. However, it remains to be seen if the cathedral anomaly will eventually dissolve in the corrosive climes of secular culture. It may be that cathedral worship is just more resistant for the time being, but ultimately on the same trajectory.

As with so many apparent facts and figures, there is in fact a richer story to read beyond mere numbers. It is important to develop more subtle skills for comprehending what is actually taking place in the apparent growth of cathedral worship. Social exchange theory can help with such interpretation. Classic cathedral worship is typically a 'low threshold' pursuit – anyone can come without any need or pressure to join a rota, group, class or other supplementary activity. However, a 'low threshold' is most likely combined with a 'high reward': the music will invariably be superb, the preaching will be consistently high, and the liturgy will be predictable and elegant.

In contrast, the dominant preferred ecclesial model in the Church of England today is 'high threshold and high reward'. The justification for this formula is usually the priority of 'discipleship', which is preferred to anything that smacks of vicarious religion, or a lack of clarity in matters of belief. 'High-Threshold-High-Reward' churches will offer attendees a rich menu and a variety of groups and activities that they will be expected to join. The committed can be identified easily enough – by the range and scale of their involvement in groups and activities. Those who are less involved will be deemed to be, by the same token, less committed. Thresholds for joining and participating are therefore set deliberately high, and this often manifests itself in areas such as restrictive practices in respect of baptisms and marriages, and can even extend, occasionally, to restricting funerals to 'members'.

The problem with the 'High-Threshold-High-Reward' churches is that, while there is a stress on discipleship and commitment, the model of church being offered is unavoidably narrow. Moreover, the concentration of resources and monies in these ecclesial paradigms means that other churches – I do not include cathedrals here – can quickly develop into 'High-Threshold-Low-Reward' churches. By that, I mean that the instinct of affirming the church as being for everyone in the community, while laudable, comes as a cost that falls only on a few. The quality and quantity of worship, pastoral ministry and more besides can only operate if a few will fund this for the many. This is by no means certain.

In terms of membership of the church, the post-war story of English Anglicanism has witnessed the slow accretion of greater density towards the wings: a density, moreover, consisting not merely of numbers but also theological and ecclesiological intensity. Both wings – depending on whether one refers to them as high and low, evangelical and catholic – have tended to be more prescriptive about what constitutes 'membership' (not only of their respective groups and societies but also wider membership of the church), and have been zealous on areas such as liturgy, reform and divisive debates, such as those on sexuality and gender. In this, 'baptism' as a means of incorporation within the church, and symbolically too in being named to broader society, has become a rite that has attracted more comprehensive ecclesial collateral.

Specifically, is 'Christening' a shared social-sacramental covenant between church and world, and God and people? Or, rather, as the high and low or evangelical and catholic wings tend to claim, a private rite, performed in public, that inducts individuals into something more obviously bounded, organizational and contained? In addressing this issue, we remain mindful of studies that speak of baptism differently, namely as the rite performed by and in the church that confers a name and social status on the child in question. So, through baptism and naming, the child becomes not only a member of the church but also a member of the broader social community.

The sociologist Mady Thung offered something of a prophetic warning to churches in her work. She noted the inevitability of churches needing to become more organized, and more like organizations, replete with plans for numerical growth and measurable impact. But Mady Thung's insights sound a further note of caution. Namely every step churches take *towards* the tighter and clearer forms of organization, coupled to overt mission and evangelism, is one further step *away* from the public at large, who, she claims, are looking for more open forms of institutional life, which offer more by way of open community than propositional clarity. Ultimately, Anglicanism's pastoral practice, mission and ministry does not have its identity rooted in being an eclectic and selective member-based organization, requiring detailed confessional subscription from believers. Anglicanism is far broader: an institutional body with many kinds of support and supporters, though with room still for those who want to regard themselves as insider subscribers.

Spirituality as the Sublime

To some extent, there are parallels between this vision of a broad church for all and the actuality of broadcasting. Michael Sadgrove put it eloquently in a recent short essay and quotes a 'convert' (I use the word advisedly) to BBC Radio Three's *Choral Evensong*. The listener writes:

> I turned on *Choral Evensong* by accident one afternoon a year or so ago and I've been listening ever since. The music is beautiful, but the special quality of Evensong lies in other places too, in the paradoxical contrast between the sinewy intricacy of sixteenth-century language, and the simplicity of the thoughts it expresses: prayers for courage, for grace, for protection from the dark, for a good death. These are things to which our minds have particularly lately turned in the aftermath of recent terrible events, but they were there all the time in the psalms and collects of Evensong. For almost 500 years the same words have been repeated by people in times of trouble or of triumph. The presence of that cloud of unseen witnesses lends an intangible quality to Choral Evensong. You could call it calm or spirituality. You could call it holiness. But it's very precious. (Michael Sadgrove, 'Evensong', *The Prayer Book Today*, pp. 11–12)

This outcome was arguably not the manifest intention of the broadcaster, but it is the outcome for the listener. So where does the mission and ministry of the church belong in such a world, and perhaps especially in contemporary English culture? Clearly, it lies in keeping space for the sacred and pastoral both possible and open, as well as alive and engaged.

In offering faith both to and for institutions, churches and clergy have a unique role in calling individuals and bodies to the horizons that lie beyond the scope of immediate priorities. The role might be said to consist of pastoral care in the present (of course), but pointing beyond the temporal and pragmatic to the world of the spiritual, the domain of values, and to the social transcendent. Indeed, churches continue to occupy and bridge the gap between created and redeemed sociality. The church holds the world before God. It is the social-sacramental skin for the community. It is not an enclave for the redeemed, but rather a resource for all those seeking meaning and truth in a world that longs for hope.

There is something about English Anglican cathedrals that can't be easily expressed in opinion. It is, arguably, more to do with atmosphere and temperament. The sheer scale of most cathedrals – their very vastness – might have something to do with their counter-cultural resilience. Perhaps they resist secularizing trends by their size and the shape of what goes on inside them. I note this telling analogy from John Milbank. A cathedral, argues Milbank, is complex, slightly contrary, encompassing space – yet *naturally* incomplete, and always pointing beyond itself to something other and higher:

> One walks through such a building conscious of continually unfolding vistas. It is a whole, yet it cannot be seen as a whole. Nor, though it is handed down to us by the past, is it ever completely finished. New spaces expressing new needs, new altars representing a multiplicity of concerns and commitments, new decorative details celebrating new ideas and discoveries, can go on being added. It is also constantly decaying and constantly being rebuilt. It can represent both diversity, and the imperfection of incompleteness, without compromising its unity or confusing its purpose. A cathedral points beyond itself. It is not definable like a city, but open to all. Its verticality is a reminder that it is not just about human beings and human relationships. It provides a complex space that can bring home to us where, as transitory, contradictory, sinful and yet ultimately hopeful and receptive human beings, we really stand before God. (John Milbank, *The Word Made Strange*, p. 284)

The honouring of values and behaviours that celebrate social affinities are rooted in a kind of 'soft' Deism, and have the character of a kind of 'low-threshold' and 'common' liturgy: all may observe and participate – through silent reverence, for example – without being specifically active in the ritual.

This should not surprise us. Remembrance Sunday is observed up and down the land with careful liturgical-pastoral choreography, and some parish churches now report that it is becoming more popular than Christmas. That said, the actual act of remembrance itself can be a curiously ambivalent religious phenomenon. Yet it is at the same time spiritually moving and socially binding – and a communion between the living and the dead, as well as a celebration of the best in humanity (i.e. noble sacrifice and virtues, etc.), albeit while reminding ourselves of humanity's darker side (i.e. violence and evil). Mausoleums that commemorate the dead of the two great wars of the twentieth century are often profoundly 'religious', even when they are not. The design and operation of apparently secular spaces often point us to the spiritual, without us knowing.

For discussion

- If the design and organization of our denomination is no longer functional or fit for purpose, what resources exist within the churches for self-correction?
- What resources exist outside churches for this, and can they be appropriate to use?
- Peter Berger and Thomas Luckmann said:

> It is important to keep in mind that the objectivity of the institutional world, however massive it may appear to the individual, is a humanly produced, constructed objectivity. (*The Social Construction of Reality*, p. 78)

> The church is too, and, given that, how should we read our denominations and congregations?

Half Term:
Extra Maths and Equations

Once the world was filled with the sacred – in thought, practice and institutional form. After the Reformation and the Renaissance, the forces of modernization swept across the globe and secularization, a corollary historical process, loosened the dominance of the sacred. In due course, the sacred shall disappear altogether except, possibly, in the private realm. (Charles Wright Mills, *The Sociological Imagination*, p. 32)

The sociological pioneers, including Weber, Durkheim, Marx and Freud, were not just theorists but also prophets of their time. They all predicted the decline of religion and its diminishing significance with the advent of industrial society. This foresight was later echoed by anthropologists, psychologists and philosophers, who argued that theological superstitions, symbolic liturgical rituals and sacred practices were all remnants of a bygone era, destined to be relegated to the private realm, as Mills had suggested.

For many sociologists, the response to the famously controversial 1966 *Time Magazine* cover, which asked 'Is God Dead?', would be 'Not yet, but he's on his way'. Among the most vocal of these proponents was Peter Berger, who linked the decline in the belief in God to the prevalence of science in the twentieth century. This shift meant that the natural phenomena which had once been interpreted in religious terms were now explained scientifically, leading to a decline in the authority of spiritual knowledge. Moreover, within religious traditions such as Protestantism, a specific rationalization had taken root. This had stripped away Catholicism's ethereal or magical functions, reducing faith to a more fundamental level, with significant societal implications.

In this evolving paradigm of Christian thought, the importance and occurrence of miracles diminished, with Protestants, in general, no longer perceiving the world as constantly influenced by divine forces. For commentators like Berger, it appeared that God was not entirely absent but had adopted a more laissez-faire approach to intervening in the world, marking a significant shift in religious beliefs.

Correspondingly, the sacred and profane were pulled further apart and began to exist in two increasingly unconnected realms that rarely delved into one another. This trajectory has largely continued to the present, with the secular and sacred pulling further apart and increasingly living separate lives. Therefore, religion's decline is linked to the advent of modernity and rationalism.

Living Apart

As the individualism of Protestantism led to an erosion of the communal basis of religious belief, rationality rendered many of its beliefs and purposes implausible and unnecessary. Two of the Galácticos who hold this viewpoint, Peter Berger and Steve Bruce, believe that religion became, in effect, a kind of lifestyle preference. An option that added value and meaning to life but did not fundamentally dictate the beginning, end and fundamental conditions of that life. Those were now determined by medicine, economics, politics and the individual's autonomy. God did not prescribe for these. As a result, churches rapidly began to yield ground to new and more communitarian or individualistic expressions of religion, such as novel forms of denominationalism, bespoke sects and other forms of religious organization that reflect the increasing individualism of life.

Through the diversity available in these options – or 'pluralism', as Berger described it – we see the fragmentation of the religious culture into a range of competing alternatives. As more significant religious expressions are accepted, the legitimations of older, more substantial faith expressions become weaker in the face of religious competition. That is, the religious routine low-level social reinforcement of objectified knowledge, which explains the social order, is drastically curtailed. For Bruce, this means that when we can no longer be sure that those we meet share our faith, we tend to keep it to ourselves.

Correspondingly, with all faiths running essentially on equal terms in modernized societies, there tends to be a lack of incentive for parents to indoctrinate children with religious beliefs. The trajectory only leads one way: a broader range of options in the religious marketplace means there are no monopolies, which in turn means that religions become a private matter of choice. In effect, a form of spiritual consumerism is created – *caveat emptor*?

In terms of maths, the number of regular givers in the Church of England fell by 30% in 2013 – a drop of 172,000 – according to the most recent statistics published by Church House, Westminster. The figures, found in *Parish Finance Statistics 2022*, make for grim reading. Income from giving, fundraising and trading was not enough to keep pace with inflation or recoup the losses of 2020 (in which parishes' income fell by 15%). Parishes' real-terms income fell by 14% between 2019 and 2022. At the same time, the Consumer Prices Index (CPI) rose by 5.4% in the 12 months to December 2021.

In total, there were 401,000 regular givers in 2021. Statistics for Mission records that, in the same year, total adult average weekly attendance was 567,000. The average weekly amount from regular givers has risen each year in recent decades, but in 2022, for the first time, this amount decreased in real terms to £16.20, from £16.80 in 2021.

In total, income was 13% lower in real terms than in 2019. Fundraising income was 31% lower, and trading income was 21% lower. But, in 2022, there was a £10-million rise in collections taken at services as churches continued to open more after the pandemic.

The report highlights the gulf between the richest and poorest parishes. In 2022, the 10% of parishes with the smallest income generated an average of £6,200 a year. For the 10% of parishes with the highest income, it was £296,000. The median income for all 12,215 parishes was £42,200, which represents a fall compared with £45,800 in 2019. Thousands of parishes are in deficit. The number of regular givers fell by 15% between 2019 and 2021. Across dioceses, the percentage of worshippers who were regular givers varied between 30% and 64%, while the level of giving ranged from £8 to £26 per week, with no correlation with deprivation.

Trends and Trajectories

That said, the trajectory of any secularization thesis in the twenty-first century needs heavy qualification, modification – or possibly even abandoning: to the point in which Berger's later work argued that secularization theory was essentially 'mistaken'. As most scholars have now recognized, there has been a rapid resurgence of religion, as religious people have either chosen to adapt or reject the perceived secularizing effects of modernity.

The growth of orthodox Islam, and particularly the continuation of religious significance in modernized states such as the USA, has refuted the thesis to an extent. However, as Grace Davie has noted, Western Europe may still be a case of exceptionalism. To paraphrase Berger himself, Europe bucks the trend and is the only place where the old secularization thesis remains in place. Yet even within Europe, the religious landscape is highly diverse. However, focusing at home, Britain (or more likely England) was described in a French study of European Religious Values as *région laïque,* meaning a high proportion of the population identified with no religious label.

Church attendance statistics in the UK regularly support this, a relatively rapid downward trajectory from half the population to only 8% in 2006. In addition, there's been a steady decline in orthodox Christian beliefs, general belief in the existence of God, and a drastic fall in religious weddings and baptisms. For Bruce, this is an obvious demonstration of the decline of organized religion in Britain, leading to a shift from religious people being loyal followers to becoming selective consumers, confirming Berger's fears of more bureaucratic practices becoming necessary and common in churches.

Therefore, and from the data, Britain is moving in line with the older, traditional secularization theses and religious people are not turning to alternatives, satisfied with having no religious label. Despite this, there has been work that has attempted to refute the evidence, much of which focuses on the belief that all people are essentially religious. In the work of Paul Heelas and Linda Woodhead, they try to locate what Bruce describes as a 'diffused spirituality' in activities such as yoga, massage therapy and other expressions of spiritual practices.

For Heelas and Woodhead, fewer than half the respondents, when questioned, claimed that their participation had anything to do with spiritual growth. However, Heelas and Woodhead still asserted that the figure they arrived at proved that the number of people in Britain who have shown interest in alternative religion is not minute. Bruce dismisses this as trivial, as the work has taken on New Age spirituality at its narrowest, and these activities are more likely to be extensions of the gym or salon rather than Christianity, practised by people who don't even pretend to see them as spiritual.

However, I think that what Bruce, Heelas and Woodhead all fail to acknowledge is the awareness of the respondents in this diffusion. The European Values Study (EVSSG) looked at a correlation between religious values and many forms of contemporary spiritual expression, the latter of which may be considered secular. That is, the spiritual origins of values which are not plainly evident to those who now hold them, or they do not hold them for religious reasons. But they were and are religious or spiritual. It is just that the holders of these values and patterns of behaviour do not recognize this. The awareness of the respondents, however, is limited.

Indications and Calculations

The indicators within the European Values Study (EVSSG) highlighted two crucial variables: first, those concerned with feelings and experiences; second, those that measured religious orthodoxy, ritual participation and institutional attachment. It would appear that in the latter's case, the study revealed a significant degree of secularization in the UK, whereas the former case shows some real persistence in religious life. For Davie, this begs the question of a permanent generational shift in religious behaviour, where we are an 'unchurched' society rather than a secular one. With markedly lower attendance and institutional detachment in the younger generation, it may be a case of 'believing without belonging'.

Counter to this, but not too dissimilar, is Danièle Hervieu-Léger's reverse characterization of the European situation as almost 'belonging without believing'. Her theory is that Western societies are less religious, not because of increasing rationality but because they are less capable of maintaining the memory of the heart of their spiritual existence. They are thus, in her words, 'amnesiac societies'. Unlike Heelas and Woodhead, who assume that the UK has found satisfactory alternatives for religion, she believes a gap needs to be filled.

Following Weber, the two crucial functions of religion are community-based and societal roles, which align with Durkheim's functional definition. The other is the offer of individual salvation. Not all religions do both. But Christianity, which did, ceded its purpose as a community base to the secular nation-state. José Casanova believes that it lost its ability to function as a religion of individual salvation. Therefore, why those people moved away from the church and did not seek alternatives is for Casanova because British people continue to be *implicit* members of their national churches, even after explicitly abandoning them.

The public becomes distant but kindly disposed supporters but does not usually seek to become active members. Moreover, they become *implicitly* religious in the process. The general view of the population, therefore, is that churches remain there as a public good which they have access to when it comes to rites of passage, birth and death. However, this is declining fast. The rates for clergy conducting baptisms, funerals and weddings are shrinking year-on-year.

That said, perhaps rather than specifically looking at the decline of religion, we should be attempting to become more attuned to new forms of religion, and specifically the implicit and vicarious nature of religious people in Britain. Therefore, it is crucial to develop a lens, or some kind of analytical instrument, through which we can view the less obvious and perhaps visible layers of British people's behaviour and commitments to understand how it is that religion still persists.

British society has both the elements of 'believing without belonging' and 'belonging without believing'. Correspondingly, it is important to try to understand those commitments that appear to be like religion in society but are, in fact, not. Equally, it is important to try to identify and understand those commitments and practices that seem to be non-religious but, in fact, are.

What is becoming clearer is that many would-be volunteers are being deterred from supporting the Church of England because of the overly onerous bureaucratic demands hoisted onto parishes. Safeguarding, vetting and training requirements for entirely non-contact roles, such as singing in a church choir, reading a lesson or leading intercessory prayer, are absurd. The demands made on churchwardens and church treasurers now mean new volunteers are needed.

The Covid-19 pandemic has evidently produced permanent scarring to most denominations in the Western world. In the Church of England, the number of regular givers is probably a more accurate estimate of regular attendance than almost any other metric. If so, the news that the Church of England is down to about 400,000 subscribers means that around 170,000 have been lost in just a decade. It is almost certain that 300,000 of the 400,000 are over the age of 50, and probably about 250,000 are over the age of 70.

Let's take a diocese like Birmingham, with a population of 1.6 million. Notably, the usual Sunday attendance (uSa) figure for the Church of England is 6,300, representing just 0.39% of the population. To put this in context, consider the football stadiums for West Bromwich Albion (capacity 25,000) and Birmingham City (capacity 29,000): Anglican worshippers in the diocese of Birmingham would not fill one stand at either football ground, let alone an entire stadium.

Given that two-thirds of the 6,300 will be retirees (in line with national figures), it will only take another decade for that figure to descend to around 2,000 – 0.13% of the population, without factoring in any growth in the city's population. That suggests that within a decade or so, the diocese will be down to about 2,000 worshippers for usual Sunday attendance (uSa). This represents a devastating statistic for England's second city and, even allowing for massive demographic changes, it has to be asked how any diocese can be sustained on such a very slender base. This is far worse than what many churchgoers assume to be an already serious scenario, namely only 3% of the population remaining in some kind of Christian congregational domain by 2030. The more likely number is less than 1%.

The national picture for the Church of England looks grim. With heavier process-led discernment and selection for ordination training, the numbers in training are currently down by 40%. Yet the Church of England knew, at the end of the twentieth century, that it was due to lose 20% of its clergy to retirement by 2025. Instead of addressing these statistics, the leadership has only watered down training, failed to keep clergy pay and pensions competitive with other caring professions, neglected to address the employment rights of its ministers, and yet tightened and lengthened its processes of recruitment.

The irony is that every step the Church of England leadership takes to look more professional only confirms how amateurish the institution really is. Small wonder that Millennials and Gen-Zers now give the churches a wide berth, and the number seeking a vocation (or career) in the Church of England looks set to decline further. Pay and pensions are barely at subsistence levels, there is no job security, and the leadership continue to enshrine and honour discrimination, inequality and poor employment practices.

Ironically, in an age of loneliness and mental health crises, Gen-Zers might be wooed to churches offering intergenerational social gatherings and making few demands for participation (https://www.politicshome.com/thehouse/article/scrolls-doom-gen-z-shunning-church).

In Scotland, the population has largely withdrawn, and now the Kirk – as it is usually dubbed – is itself withdrawing. Its finances are stretched, new ministers are scarce and congregations scarcer. The Edinburgh headquarters of the Church of Scotland has done some research, crunched some numbers and formed webs of committees to determine the cull. The results now emerging from the committees are only just beginning to bite, but Church of Scotland HQ have decreed swingeing cuts in the Kirk. Church of Scotland churches presently number around 4,500. The plan is to reduce this number by 40%, and the ministers and the manse-stock by the same percentage.

Is this fiscal prudence or merely an organized retreat in the face of rapid secularization? In 2001, 65% of Scottish people claimed to have Christian affiliation, with 33% saying they either had no religion or would not state it. Jewish, Hindu, Sikh, Muslim and other faiths made up the remaining 2%. By 2011, Christian affiliation had shrunk to 54%, and those with no religion was 47%. The Muslim population in the same decade had grown from 0.8% to 1.45%.

We should note, incidentally, that across Europe 30% of live births in 2020 were to parents citing a religious but non-Christian background. Most of the 30% will be Muslim, though Hindu and Sikh will be prominent too. This represents a seismic shift in the religious heritage of modern Europe. Irrespective of whether those of Islamic heritage will claim to be 'secular Muslims' in due course, Europe is no longer a predominantly Christian continent. There are now more agnostics, 'nones' and people of non-Christian faith than those claiming Christian heritage.

Perhaps that is part of the reason why the figures for church weddings in Scotland also paint a bleak picture. In 1970, churches were close to 31,000 solemnizations of marriage. By 1990 that had dropped to just over 20,000. In 2020, the figure was 5,333, with 6,653 civil weddings. It turns out that 2005 was the year when there were more civil marriages than Christian ceremonies. In 1970, the Church of Scotland performed around 35,500 baptisms. In 2020, the figure was 459. Figures for the Church of England in the same period show almost 350,000 infant baptisms in 1970, but by 2020 the number had fallen to just over 40,000.

The story of Scotland's statistics reflects broader trends. Judaism is declining, but at a much slower rate than church affiliation. Islam is growing, but still accounts for less than 2% of the population. Sikhism and Hinduism are largely stable, but remain numerically small. The diaspora churches have grown, but it is unclear how much of this is 'transfer growth' – moving from one denomination or congregation to another. Despite their apparent and impressive growth, it will take at least one more generation to ascertain the long-term stability of new churches.

As we can see from the tables below relating to the Anglican Church of Canada, the maths is challenging and the equations are a major cause for concern. Research from Neil Elliot on metrics of church size including electoral rolls and distinct identifiable donation sources show membership dropping by about 10% nationwide during 2020, and data from 2021 confirming a similar decrease (https://anglicanjournal.com/data-show-membership-falling-10-per-cent-each-year-during-2020-and-2021-church-statistician/ and https://anglican.ink/2024/05/03/canadian-church-membership-decline-steepens/#google_vignette).

HALF-TERM: EXTRA MATHS AND EQUATIONS

Anglican Church of Canada Annual Statistics, 2019–20

	Bishops: Active	Priests: Paid	Priests: Unpaid	Deacons: Paid	Deacons: Unpaid	Diocesan Paid workers
Algoma	1	26	15	5	4	5
Arctic	4	12	3	2	11	2.5
Athabasca	1	6	0	0	6	1
Brandon	1	14	9	0	11	2
British Columbia	1	55	1	0	0	21
Caledonia	1	5	8	0	1	1
Calgary	1	44	14	5	17	11
Central Newfoundland	1	18	1	2	6	1
Eastern Newfoundland and Labrador	1	37	4	1	22	5
Edmonton	1	43	3	2	9	4
Fredericton	1	55	11	1	10	7
Huron	1	137	0	2	30	12
Kootenay	1	17	10	1	5	5
Mishamikoweesh	2	0	44	0	4	5
Montreal	1	39	9	0	10	11
Moosonee	1	6	4	7	1	0
New Westminster	1	82	11	0	21	10
Niagara	2	75	0	0	15	25
Nova Scotia and PEI	1	87	5	0	10	8
Ontario	1	34	16	0	4	9
Ottawa	1	80	0	3	1	16
Qu'Appelle	1	9	12	0	9	4
Quebec	1	9	16	2	0	0
Rupert's Land	3	30	18	2	10	6
Saskatchewan	2	9	7	1	9	2
Saskatoon	1	18	6	0	0	1
Territory of the People	1	8	0	0	0	5
Toronto	3	212	107	0	51	44
Western Newfoundland	0	23	0	4	3	1
Yukon	1	4	3	0	5	1
Total	39	1,194	337	40	285	225.5

THE EXILED CHURCH

	Number of parishes	Total number on parish rolls*	Average Sunday attendance	Regular identifiable givers	Area of diocese (sq. km)
Algoma	52	5,053	923	3,374	112,000
Arctic	48	33,889	1,808	1,745	3,885,000
Athabasca	17	896	306	475	414,400
Brandon	25	2,935	337	622	259,000
British Columbia	45	4,890	2,200	3,100	32,000
Caledonia	20	1,048	405	326	433,000
Calgary	67	7,523	2,496	3,266	212,380
Central Newfoundland	27	9,375	2,642	6,888	69,930
Eastern Newfoundland and Labrador	39	21,053	1,600	6,408	317,000
Edmonton	44	5,912	1,417	2,381	77,900
Fredericton	72	9,823	2,373	4,248	71,300
Huron	124	21,000	6,000	10,000	31,000
Kootenay	26	2,363	840	1,197	215,000
Mishamikoweesh	28	14,000	900	100	250,000
Montreal	68	7,017	3,405	3,417	21,300
Moosonee	21	14,219	350	400	560,000
New Westminster	63	9,952	3,296	4,472	77,700
Niagara	80	12,967	3,916	6,934	8,600
Nova Scotia and PEI	94	21,892	5,126	7,845	61,000
Ontario	46	5,896	2,261	2,613	17,700
Ottawa	68	8,809	2,277	5,500	46,600
Qu'Appelle	26	2,727	852	853	197,000
Quebec	65	1,586	375	804	720,000
Rupert's Land	52	4,215	1,608	1,865	150,000
Saskatchewan	22	8,417	915	439	350,000
Saskatoon	19	1,500	525	620	76,000
Territory of the People	19	1,005	295	347	168,350
Toronto	178	37,646	13,810	13,786	26,000
Western Newfoundland	30	16,360	1,394	6,839	60,000
Yukon	13	963	122	114	300,000
Total	1,498	294,931	64,774	100,978	9,220,160

* The basis for this number varies substantially between dioceses.

I've picked the Anglican Church of Canada here because of the numbers. There are just under 1,500 parishes in the entire province. And there are just under 1,500 paid employees on the payroll for a uSa of 65,000. That means for every 43 attendees, there is an employee. While it is true that almost 300,000 claim affiliation, only 100,000 are financially supporting the mission and ministry of the Province. The Province consists of 5.7 million square miles (9.2 million square km), which averages out as one salaried church worker per 3,800 square miles. Or, just one for an area the same size as Cornwall, Devon and Somerset combined. Even by concentrating resources and personnel in the areas that are most densely populated, it would be obvious that any meaningful claim on national coverage will be tendentious.

Summary – Save the Parish?

At the time of writing, the Church of England Diocese of Truro (Cornwall) has more personnel working in diocesan HQ than feet on the ground in parishes and chaplaincies. Suppose this trend is being replicated across the Church of England. In that case, a situation will quickly evolve whereby there will 40-plus regional HQs, 120-plus staffed episcopal residences, two central London head offices (Church House Westminster and Lambeth Palace) but no staffed local outlets. As a business model, it doesn't take a genius to see that this is a recipe for bankruptcy. Suppose the 'core business' of the church is local pastoral care and outreach. In that case, it is also evident that the regional HQs are not places to which the population will naturally turn in order to find the help, comfort and support they might be seeking.

At this halfway stage of our curriculum, we can make tentative suggestions about what lies ahead for the churches and faith communities. Here again, though I draw on Scottish data, local knowledge, interviews and conversations, the broad trends appear to be as follows.

First, religious literacy is in decline throughout public life. In broadcast and print media, there is less interest and investment in what faith communities are engaged in within the public sphere. Where religion is reported, often it will be some examples of extremism, fundamentalism or motivated violence. Or another tale in the long litany of child sexual abuse.

Second, there is less religious literacy in schooling, as we have already noted. This will make it harder and harder for all faith traditions to reach and recruit beyond their familial and community networks.

Furthermore, the current generation of believers (again, in any tradition) are struggling to pass their faith on to the next generation.

Third, the only groups managing – now – to pass on faith traditions and beliefs to the next generation are small in number and ethnically distinct (Muslim, Hindu, Jewish, etc.). But even here, there is evidence of organic depletion and decline (e.g. Jewish). And even where the numbers indicate growth (e.g. Islam), the quality of belief being passed on is thinner and more diluted. Few third-generation Muslims read the Qur'an in Arabic (as taught), or take Hajj to Mecca, but may observe Eid.

Fourth, the decomposition of beliefs and practices is already advanced in Christian practice. As we have noted, few will regard Ascension Day (always a Thursday) as a day of 'obligation'. The festival, called not so long ago 'Holy Thursday', has now slipped into 'Ascensiontide' and will be celebrated on the nearest Sunday. Here, churches merely demonstrate reasonable adjustments to the demands of weekends and working life. Similar adjustments can be observed over Ramadan for Muslims working in essential services.

Fifth, as the presence of churches and other places of worship for faith communities continues to recede in public life, expressions of religion that market and brand themselves differently from the rest are likely to enjoy greater visibility and audibility in a crowded consumer marketplace and so will most likely experience a 'bounce' in membership. However, market forces and consumer trends also show that it is becoming increasingly hard for such faith communities to continue growing exponentially. Several charismatic and evangelical church movements are currently experiencing a flat-lining in growth. New and novel initiatives that once punctuated congregational life with regular spiritual fillips are now often met with low-level disenchantment and ennui, and not with renewed intensification, let alone revival.

Sixth, there is a crisis with clergy. The 'priest factories' of Ireland are largely closed (just one seminary now), and across Britain, recruitment into full-time ordained or licensed ministry is in steep decline. The Church of Scotland struggles to recruit new ministers, as it can no longer guarantee roles for their clergy after the initial period of service following training. The average age of clergy in the Church of England continues to rise, with greater numbers offering to minister unpaid in later life, or even in retirement. The writing was on the wall half a century ago. As Loren Mead showed, the maths is clear. In the 1950s, the average seminarian in the USA (across all denominations) would serve out 40-plus years of ministry after training, education and ordination. By 1990, the average length of service post-ordination had slipped to around 25-plus years. In the twenty-first century, it is under 20 years. This makes theological education and training more expensive – the same investment for less return. Most denominations lack self-awareness here, and so unconsciously reduce the length, cost and quality of ordination training to adjust. The result is an inevitable decline in quality and professional esteem, which makes it less appealing for vocations, and so harder to recruit.

Seventh, if clergy now 'come cheap' (so to speak) or even cost-free, fewer will seek ordained ministry if the leadership, in order to compensate for the growing deficits in the provision, is now being plugged by unpaid volunteers. In 1955, the ratio of Episcopalian vacancies to seminarians in the USA was 1:1. By 1990, the ratio was 1:2, meaning that half of those who were seminarians were facing the prospect of undertaking their ordained ministry and work unpaid. In the twenty-first century, the supply–demand equations have become more acute for those in ordination training, or coming to the end of their initial period of ministry (i.e. curacy). With no guarantee of further paid ministry, the 'ordination market' becomes nervy, insecure and prone to more risks for candidates.

Eighth, as we have already noted, secularization is inside faith communities and is acting as a soft regulative framework for believers in relation to the time, energy, resources, commitment and financial support they are prepared to offer a congregation or denomination. Furthermore, when the 'local supply' of the 'core business' is reduced, relocated or dislocated, it is rare for the faithful to recalibrate their belonging. At this point, hitherto regular and committed believers may cease to invest in religion as before and turn to forms of spirituality that meet their immediate needs. There is a limit, obviously, to how far people will travel and stretch themselves to attend their 'local' place of worship. If it is too far away and is no longer meaningfully local, religiously minded folks will find other ways to secure the care, comfort, peace, spiritual nourishment and stimulation they seek.

Ninth, the strong pulse of the 'seeker-factor' in contemporary spirituality shows that secularization has a limited range in modernity. However, that does not necessarily mean that churches will be beneficiaries. As Jim Davis and Michael Graham note, evangelicals are now experiencing the early signs of the (proverbial) harsh winters that lie ahead. Faith is not being passed on down the generations, and younger people cite culture wars, lack of inclusivity and generosity, inability to listen and engage with other positions, and attitudes to racism, sexism and homophobia as the main reasons they stay away from their parents' churches. There are other puzzles, too, in the statistics. Divorce rates among ex-evangelical churchgoers are markedly lower than those who opt to stay 'churched'. Lines of fracture are no longer on doctrine but rather on attitudes to sexual freedom, other faiths, politics, personal wealth and economics.

Tenth, and finally, while Pentecostal Christianity seems to be sweeping all before it, the truth for the Western world is that while many are queuing at the front door of such churches, significant numbers are also leaving by the back door.

Yet, religion is not disappearing from the landscape so much as being transformed before our very eyes. The modern world is not secular. It remains spiritual, and with every indication that the effervescence and creativity of spirituality is growing and extensive. In contrast, official institutional religion is declining fast, and its leaders and organizations are less trusted than ever before.

For discussion

- Given the numbers discussed in this extra lesson on maths, what might constitute a way forward for denominations as they seek to balance their books? How does this impact your local church?
- Although the statistics look bleak, where does hope lie going forward? Where will the leadership for change come from, and how can it be supported?
- Bill Clinton said: 'It's the economy, stupid.' This phrase is often attributed to Clinton in 1992, though it was actually coined by James Carville, the strategist credited with the Democrats' successful 1992 election win over George Bush. James Carville's other phrases were 'Change versus More of the Same' and 'Don't Forget Health Care'. Take these three phrases together and devise an election strategy for a new leader in your denomination.

Lesson Six:
Science

The most important thing to state at the start of this lesson is that science may not play much of a role in future trends towards secularization. One could argue that theories of evolution, geology and natural sciences in the eighteenth and nineteenth centuries undermined confidence in biblical authority. One could argue that advances in medicine, physics, biology and chemistry undermined confidence in divine action in the same period. Certainly, a major feature in the story of nineteenth–twentieth-century evangelical apologetics has seen preachers and teachers trying to re-establish biblical authority as a rival to or complementary of scientific knowledge.

But the twenty-first century is playing out rather differently. The merging generation of evangelicals are unlikely to regard the Bible as an ancient science textbook that can take on Charles Darwin or, for that matter, the cosmology of Carl Sagan. It is far more likely that if – and it is an if – evangelical youth have any knowledge of scripture at all, it will be rooted in what feeds their personal spirituality rather than settling a science versus religion argument. As King Wuling of Zhao (died 295 BC) famously observed, 'A talent for following the ways of yesterday is insufficient to improve today's world.' In the annals of all strategic thinking, the most common error is to 'fight the last war', preparing uselessly for old challenges rather than gearing up for the future.

In 1929, Lieutenant Colonel J. L. Schley of the Corps of Engineers wrote in *The Military Engineer*: 'It has been said critically that there is a tendency in many armies to spend the peacetime studying how to fight the last war.' The same sentiments have been repeated ever since: 'Peacetime generals are always fighting the last war instead of the next one.' To some extent, the entire 'science' of the combat strategy of churches in their attempts to face (or fight?) secularization is an exemplar of this. As though trouncing Darwin or Dawkins would make any difference to the emerging generation of agnostics and sceptics. It seems unlikely.

Gen-Z

What does the natural landscape of generational belief look like in the twenty-first century? Well, different. 'Generation Z' is one of several terms used to describe post-millennial youth born after 1996. According to some social scientists, they may prefer juice bars to pub crawls, and rank quality family time ahead of sex; and possibly prioritize good grades before friendship. Gen-Zers are more likely to document their lives through Instagram and Snapchat – creating an audience for their lives who are immediately interacting. Somehow, sharing the image of a plate of food with a hundred other 'friends' is a 'social connection', helping to combat alienation and engendering a form of socialization.

As the former head of an Oxford College, I noted that it was commonplace for many of my colleagues to assume that Gen-Zers lacked emotional and mental resilience. There is anecdotal evidence for this view. A neighbouring college flagged a new 'resilience initiative' for its undergraduates and encouraged all new students to attend. But the older undergraduate body responded with criticism, saying they were '*hurt* by the implication that they lacked resilience'. Yet, while this might seem to be the case on the surface – Gen-Zers are less emotionally tough, and seemingly more easily hurt – I hold that the picture is slightly more subtle.

Gen-Zers are more sensitive to balance than previous generations. In practice, this means that they are less inclined to discrimination of any kind and broadly committed to equality – in gender, sexuality, ethnicity and any 'protected characteristic' (e.g. disability) – being taken as read. It is rare to hear an undergraduate making a joke that could be construed as sexist or racist, for example. But such humour was commonplace in my childhood – as even the seemingly innocuous 'there was an Irishman, Scotsman, Welshman, Englishman …' jokes testified. One is just as likely to be censured for the sexism of such jokes today as for the 'man' reference and for the stereotyping of cultures and nations. Gen-Zers will be (almost incurably) 'nice', and, with that, *almost* Christian (but not quite). This is the essence of Kenda Creasy Dean's fine *Almost Christian*.

I also noticed a shift from dispositional to episodic patterns of participation and belonging in undergraduates. They do not identify closely with or become members of institutions, groups, political parties, churches or other organizations. They will go to an event and may regard that as significant. But regular commitment to a group or body is less apparent. They may join movements – but these tend to be 'seasonal' or limited to specific issues. They may join a gym, to be sure, but this is contractual, and it does not usually require anything other than the exercise of their consumerist assent.

So, the concept of long-term membership of a group, institution or organization has become rather more attenuated for Gen-Zers. They are less likely to join a political party or trade union. But they may join a movement like Momentum – a British 'grassroots' political organization founded in 2015 that supports the Labour Party. Their engagement with value-based institutions will be occasional and consumerist rather than unequivocally committed. In ecclesial terms, joining a vogue-ish and niche 'Fresh Expression' for a season is more likely to appeal than lifelong membership of a denomination or congregation. Gratifying personal spiritual experience will come before collective duty towards or affiliation within an institution.

Somehow, to borrow the sociological trope of Grace Davie, 'believing without belonging' has attained a new podium among Gen-Zers. They tend to be spiritual, but not religious. And when they do turn up for any religious event or service, agreement or solidarity with the underpinning ethos or beliefs should not be taken at face value. Numbers do not mean what they used to any more. A hundred undergraduates attending a moody, sentient candlelit compline service in the college chapel tells us little about the condition of their souls, or the state of belief of any of the attendees. If those numbers ever did, of course.

Our cultural landscape in the West is unusual to comprehend. Our world is not one of secularism or secularization. The twenty-first century is turning out to be stubbornly religious, in which absorption with anything from spirituality to fundamentalism is seldom far from the news. However, we appear to have moved from a culture of assumption to one of consumption – with religion now a *choice*. As Dean notes, we are witnessing the rise of the 'nones': no longer atheists or agnostics; or Church of England by default; or Jewish because their parents were. Millennials, when asked what religion they follow, typically tick 'none'. The emerging generation is SBNR – spiritual, but not religious.

Noncommittal, Yet Committed

According to the Pew Research Center (2014, http://www.pewforum.org – Pew Report on America's Religious Landscape), formal attachment to religious organizations in the USA is in decline and 'no affiliation' is increasingly reported. Similarly, 'nones' now comprise a significant percentage of the UK population (perhaps up to a third) and over 75% of those under 25. But – and this is a big 'but' – many 'nones' *do* profess to believe in God. Yet they freely confess to doing little about it. The shifting cultural landscape is, therefore, this: Personal, Therapeutic Moralistic Deism is on the rise. The emerging generation is kind, considerate, tolerant and good. It will not stand for racism, sexism, homophobia or xenophobia. The emerging generation believes in many good things, and also in God, but does not join a faith organization to express this.

I offer some asides by comment here, as both an academic and a clergyperson. I am not much worried about the reduction in numbers where Christianity is concerned. History and sociology teach us that such things ebb and flow. I am far more concerned about the qualitative factor: what *kind* of Christianity are we talking about? It is not so much that Christianity is being secularized. Rather, more subtly, Christianity is mutating into a much broader, but also 'thinner' version of itself. Another way of labelling 'moralistic Deism' is to say we are seeing the rise of the 'Almost Christian', as Dean notes; being religious is being replaced by being nice. This might explain why, on a visit to a school some years ago, I noted the school's core values: no bullying; respect for all; recycle everything. One cannot quibble with this. But these values are not exactly the pillars of Western civilization. They are not the Ten Commandments.

Robert Putnam has noted the collapse of voluntary institutions and neighbourly connections, with implied implications for religious patterns of belonging. Putnam's more recent work charts the alarming acceleration of individualism in American society, which in turn lays the foundation for less corporate religion and belief, and greater emphasis on personal spirituality. The landscape, then, is changing fast.

Churches and other religious congregations are like marooned islets in an ever-rising globally warmed sea of individualism and personal spirituality. The 'we' generation has morphed, arguably, into 'generation me'.

Thus, today's teenagers tend to view God as either a butler or a therapist, someone who meets their needs when summoned ('a cosmic lifeguard', as one youth minister put it) or who listens non-judgementally and helps youth feel good about themselves ('kind of like my guidance counsellor', according to one student). Most young people (even non-religious ones) believe that religion has much to offer, and those who attend church tend to feel positively about their congregations even when they are critical of religion in general.

Many teenagers say that religion benefits individuals or society, or both. The bad news for churches, arguably, is the reason teenagers are not *hostile* towards religion: they just seem not to care about it very much. Religion is not a big deal to them. Most US teenagers tend to be quite inarticulate about the faith, religious beliefs and practices that they have, and the meaning or place they may have in their lives.

In a telling analogy, Dean argues that religion has moved from being a matter of bounded, propositional or behavioural 'territory', in which people locate themselves as 'in' or 'out', or perhaps 'on the fence'. Instead, faith has become something more akin to the proverbial African farm – one in which the landscape is vast and boundless. In other words, there is no fence at all. The only question to ask therefore is this: are you moving closer to the farmhouse, or further away? This is a kind of detachment from formal obligations and the logical outworking of a religious ecology that is consumption-based, not assumption-grounded.

This is a new landscape, to be sure. But what is the ground of its being? Dean argues that 'niceness' is the new faith; and because there is little in the way of antidote to niceness, 'nones' are growing in number, across the generations. That said, 'nones' do value religion as being personally useful: in addition to helping people be nicer and feel better about themselves, religion can provide comfort amid turmoil and support for decisions that (by and large) teenagers want to make anyway. Otherwise, explicit and propositional faith stays in the background. (Perhaps it is 'not nice' to share this faith any more, unless asked?)

Moralistic Therapeutic Deism has little to do with an immanent God or a sense of a divine mission in the world. It offers comfort, bolsters self-esteem, helps solve problems and lubricates interpersonal relationships by encouraging people to do good, feel good and keep God at arm's length. It is a kind of self-emolliating spirituality; its thrust is personal happiness and helping people treat each other nicely.

Funeral for a Friend

I suspect that the litmus test for assessing the extent of generational change and its implications for mission can probably be best understood by speculating about death and memorialization in the future. If our cultural commentators – who speak of 'gospel amnesia' and 'a thoroughgoing fragmentation in lineage of Christian memory' – are right, then what will a funeral visit by a clergyperson look like in 2050? Until recently, many Christian ministers conducting funerals could have been reasonably confident that, unless otherwise requested, there would be hymns and prayers at the ceremony. The Lord's Prayer might be said, some hymns – many learned at school – might be sung, and perhaps certain passages of scripture and collects might be included and familiar to a number of the mourners.

But what of the future, where prayers, collects and hymns are not likely to have been part of their schooling for most mourners? What types of religious sentiment will be uttered by the generation that is, in all probability, non-conversant in the language of formal religion, but fluent in the many dialects of spirituality?

Recent research led by Margaret Holloway at the University of Hull identified a marked shift in funerals and memorialization (https://rememberm eproject.wordpress.com/the-project/). The approach to death in the UK is changing fast. Religious funerals are perceived to be inflexible, impersonal and overly formal. There is a growing trend for funerals and memorial services to be flexible, life-affirming (if not life-celebrating), bespoke, inclusive and hybrid in character. Funerals and memorial services can draw on resources rooted in religious traditions.

Still, the practice of an entire funeral being an approved expression of that religious tradition seems to be in decline. There is ample anecdotal evidence of traditional memorials rapidly giving way to, and now co-existing with, a developing range of alternative forms of remembering the deceased. Moreover, the bereaved are choosing to use public spaces quite differently as they memorialize the departed – including founding charities, online memorials, or sharing meaningful rituals in significant open spaces (e.g. beaches, woodlands, hilltops), as well as marking deaths at park benches, roadside shrines and other places.

At the end of the twentieth century, in an article for the *Harvard Business Review*, Joseph Pine and James Gilmore suggested that the 'experience economy' would emerge as a key cultural change in the new millennium. By this, the authors pointed towards new patterns of spending among Millennials. The emerging generation would focus less on quantity and more on quality, less on material acquisition and more on personal attainment. In practical terms, this means less spending on consumer goods and more spending on lifestyle: eating, entertainment and 'experiences'. 'Experience', Gilmore and Pine argued, would become a distinct quantifiable economic reality and have its own power, and it would incorporate yoga, gym, travel – and religion.

This is in no way a critical remark, but I suspect that the stress on 'experience' is one of the overwhelming cultural changes to be seen in the twenty-first century. And 'experience' is essentially a celebration of life. It turns an individual mourning into a moment of personal loss to be reflected upon, individualized and then shared on social media. Indeed, such change is arguably already upon us.

Increasingly, ministers find themselves under soft socio-cultural pressure to provide a ceremony that celebrates the life of the deceased person and does not major on the actual mourning and loss that death brings. I presided at one such quite recently, and a mourner on leaving remarked that none of the tributes had mentioned the fact that the individual we were remembering and mourning had in fact died. Indeed, were it not for my own address and use of traditional prayers and scriptural sentences, death would not have been mentioned at all.

I recall attending a recent funeral for a young mother who had tragically died giving birth to her third child, leaving behind two children under five and a husband about 30 years of age. While this may still be relatively commonplace in the developing world and would not have been entirely strange to most Britons barely a century ago, advances in healthcare make such occurrences extremely rare today. At the crematorium, we celebrated the mother's life. A symbolic centrepiece of the funeral was the coffin: not simply bearing the body of the young mother, but beautifully, hauntingly and somewhat incongruously painted and decorated with the favourite animated-cartoon characters that she and her children had enjoyed when watching TV together.

The coffin had become a kind of toy chest, the type of furniture one might covet for a nursery. The funeral was presided over by a Humanist minister, who began the celebration of the mother's life with an affirmation that all faiths were equal and valuable, and that those who had come to the crematorium with no kind of faith were equally welcome. Nothing was void; equality of experience was assumed. All the mourners wore bright colours, and the importance of this being a positive day to experience and remember was stressed.

Humans are a social, meaning-making species. Faced with death, birth and rites of passage, religion and spirituality still have their futures. And in all likelihood, the funeral of the future will be able to tell us just how much change has passed between our generations. And a pentimento of the present suggests an emerging, future picture. I suspect that the religious-spiritual landscape we are now plotting has less content and more feeling. It will have far fewer propositions, and more performative relationality. It will leave memorable experiences, but far less to remember by rote. It will be less prohibitive, and more permissive.

Funerals, for the foreseeable future, will be broader moments of shared memorialization and experience. Shared on social media, mediated through multi-media, they will be more spiritual and less religious.

But interestingly, I suspect, less alienating and more empowering for mourners. There will be gaps in knowledge and memory, to be sure; but becoming generations have always found a way through to the past. There is no reason to suppose that Millennials and Gen-Zers will lack the wisdom and the tenacity to do likewise.

Summary

Religion is a chain of memory. Stretched and, perhaps in some places, threadbare and even broken, it is a chain, nonetheless. I suspect that religion is merely *mutating* into significant forms of personal spirituality, rather than disappearing:

> spirituality ... has moved from the self-spirituality of the boomer generation to a more aesthetic spirituality, a spirituality that is focused on pleasure and experience in and of itself ... Successful churches, it seems, offer an atmosphere and intimate experience of God over and above doctrine ... the spirituality of intimacy of the millennial generation will be deeply bound up with the consumerism that has increasingly concerned youth throughout the post-war period.' (Sylvia Collins, 'Spirituality and Youth', in Martyn Percy, *Calling Time*, pp. 233–5)

The added power of consumerism at the present time reinforces this sense: niche marketing to almost every age group for every stage of life is not only prevalent but also highly successful. In times of social upheaval and cultural discontinuity especially, generations tend to become more sharply set off from one another. (We see this as I write in the so-called 'Brexit' debate, arguably, as much as we do in religious beliefs and practices.) And in the emerging faith of Millennials and Gen-Z, although desires appear to be still clustered around spiritual fulfilment and 'personal experience', there is also a craving for 'the authentic'. There is a hunger for authenticity, for correspondence between one's outer and inner lives – a desire to break through into a more spacious and nourishing conception of the common life we all share.

I suspect that, increasingly, we shall see Millennials and Gen-Zers treating religion as an issue – albeit an important one – but mindful of the perceived pathologies of religious belief and practice (fundamentalism, discrimination, violence, etc.). With religion seen as a repository for problematic beliefs and practices, the field is clear for individualist spirituality to become the ascendant. My sketch of this emerging, shifting landscape, then, appears to be pointing towards the foregrounding of personal experience and spiritual fulfilment, and suggests that formal and traditional religion is consigned further into the background. At present, it is hard to see a different picture emerging. But then, even 50 years ago, few would have predicted a sketch of such a landscape at all.

For discussion

- If science is no longer a threat to religious belief, how should Christians engage with issues such as AI, climate change, gene therapy, etc?
- What can science teach religions about awe, wonder, truth, morality, research and humility?
- Charles Wright Mills suggested: 'The sociological imagination enables its processor to understand the larger historical scene in terms of its meaning for the inner life and the external career of a variety of individuals ...' (*The Sociological Imagination*, p. 5). In the light of Mills' observation, how do you process the past, present and future of your local church?

Lesson Seven: Politics and Economics

Being rather old-school, I cannot see how economics and politics can be understood without high proficiency in maths. A key issue in the process of self-secularization that many churches have unwittingly embarked upon lies in the subtle yet insidious ways that churches and faith communities have been seduced into colluding with consumerism. As Robert Bellah noted, multiple-choice ('niche spirituality') suggests the possibility of over 220 million American religions – one for each of us. Yet the very possibility of choice (over and against obligation) puts the survival of the community of memory at risk – and to be replaced by 'empathetic sharing' by loosely associated individuals and networks. Under such conditions, faith can quickly become privatized; the property of a sect that sees itself engaged with but apart from society.

Thus, faith becomes 'overspecialized' in the sector, and what Bellah terms 'quasi-therapeutic blandness' quickly sets in, which cannot resist competition with more vigorous forms of radical religious individualism, replete with their dramatic claims of self-realization or the resurgent religious conservatism that spells out clear, if simple, answers in an increasingly bewildering world. True, churches have not been slow to attract spiritual consumers hunting for meaning and fulfilment. But Christian faith might be more about subtraction than addition.

User-friendly Faith

Peter Schmiechen in *Saving Power* perceptively points out that the emphasis on pragmatism (or technique) and consumerism in American Christianity creates a range of problems:

> one is that the techniques can be borrowed from general organizational theory and marketing strategies and have no goal other than

meeting people's needs as a way of expanding membership. This opens the door to the great debate over what are legitimate and illegitimate needs for religious communities to meet. While Jesus Christ does in fact meet our heartfelt and deepest needs, in America the gospel too often has become a technique for self-improvement and personal happiness. (p. 38)

Such 'user-friendly' forms of religion abound in America, and increasingly in other developed nations too. Schmiechen, at the time of writing, would have had in mind church-growth movements such as Willow Creek and also the writings of Rick Warren (i.e. *The Purpose Driven Life*, etc.), or the 'boom-and-bust' wonder years of John Wimber's 'Signs, Wonders and Church Growth'. These are effectively marketed and consumed as ecclesial steroids, with the promise of rapid growth, increased strength, and gains in weight and appearance. The body of Christ gets beefed up, so to speak.

The common thread is the promotion of religion as something that will solve problems and improve the lives of individuals. Or, that churches looking to be stronger, fitter, bigger, better and more appealing have a shortcut that bypasses the slog of 'no pain, no gain'. Like miracle diets, the appeal lies in instantaneous attainment and accomplishment. The highly successful publications of Rick Warren appear to emphasize God's purposes for the individual. However, nagging questions remain. Are churches and individuals being asked to give their lives to God's purposes? Or is God's alleged purpose simply a veneer of techniques to enhance the quest for meaning and success?

Complexity and Simplicity

The religious economy is complex, to be sure – much like that of religious geography. One of the leading commentators on religion and politics in the USA is Robert P. Jones (*The End of White Christian America* and *White Too Long*), who is the CEO of the Public Religion Research Institute (PRRI). His recent books on the churches and racism have rightly attracted high praise for their depth of research, the range of statistics he draws on, and the bodies he consults (The Pew Foundation, several Washington DC-based polling and research centres, etc.). Best of all, perhaps, is his unimpeachable clarity: the boldness and frankness of his prescient analysis; and his conclusions and future projections.

Few could easily argue with Jones' devastating blend of data, history, cultural and political analysis, and nuanced feel for and understanding of religion in contemporary America. Granted, American Christianity has evolved differently from its European forebears. In the USA, the customer is king. Faith thrives on religious consumerism. It is also financed differently, with congregations mostly paying their own way for their own plant, staffing and resourcing. Even in classic 'mainline' denominations (Methodist, Presbyterian, Baptist, Episcopalian, etc.), individual congregations tend to set their budgets and pay their clergy, hiring and firing at will.

On a fact-finding trip some years ago now, researching how the organizational and managerial infrastructure in a historic Episcopalian diocese operated, I was struck by the difference between expectations, and where the power in The Episcopal Church resided, compared to the British Anglican churches. This USA diocese was a well-run enterprise, but there were very few diocesan staff. Congregations (still called parishes, but not in the sense Europeans mean) that reached out to young people hired their youth ministers. The bishop could not understand why you would need a Diocesan Youth Advisor or why every Church of England diocese might.

The conversation with the bishop produced the same shrug of the shoulders for paid officers for mission, evangelism, stewardship, ethnicity, disability, ethical investment and more. Congregations that had a vision for such a ministry got on with it. They did not wait for their bishop or diocese to organize it. Those that did not offer a panoply of ministries – perhaps a small rural church dozens of miles from anywhere – were working out something different, like how to care for immigrant crop workers.

Parishes raised their funds and, for the most part, kept the vast majority of what they raised for their local mission. The quota paid into central funds was minuscule – a notional 5%–8%, depending on need. Most of what the quota was collected for went to subsidized parishes that needed ministry support but could not afford it and probably never would.

The number of diocesan employees the bishop had at his disposal could be numbered on the fingers of two hands. The central resourcing from the diocese to the congregations comprised some legal advisors, some HR and mediation experts competent in resolving intra-congregational conflict, and some administration, including financial. The bishop did not think it was strange that more than a third of his congregations had staffing levels greater than the diocese. Or that many of his clergy were paid more than him.

More recently, the diocese mothballed its cathedral for various reasons, including financial. As the bishop could not justify subsidizing a cathedral that had become insolvent, the diverse ministries in that city are now shared between the neighbouring parishes. Meanwhile, the cathedral remains open, but its role in ministry will be rekindled only when the culture of the city and its demographics change.

While I am not suggesting for a moment that the American model translates to Europe, the refreshing pragmatism of the USA Episcopalian dioceses is mirrored in other mainline denominations. Bishops are, therefore, left to function as the Ordinal requires: caring for the clergy, teaching through scholarship and study, speaking out on behalf of the voiceless, and only when necessary speaking for the diocese too. My US bishop colleague was bewildered by my description of the episcopal and diocesan portfolios and expectations in England. 'No one would fund that here ... or expect a diocese to provide those services,' he said.

English Anglican white evangelicals probably think that the analysis of Robert P. Jones represents a range of subjects on which they'd rather not comment (i.e. 'Let's just get back to those Mission Action Plans, church-plant, grow, grow, grow ...', etc.). But Jones has done some more calculations and projections for us to wrestle with. As he is charting the deep and rapid changes in the cultural currents, his data and research should give yet more cause for concern to white evangelicals in the UK and USA.

Deceptive Trends

We have known for some time that evangelicalism still seems to be the best at attracting young people to church. Evangelicals have indeed assumed this. They usually go one step further, making the logical deduction that more young people must mean the future of the church also belongs to evangelicals.

But appearances can be deceptive, and this hubris has been checked in the first quarter of this century by the rapid fluxes of culture change among evangelical youth. They are not necessarily against equal marriage, likely to have gay and lesbian friends, and likely to have friends who are Muslim, Hindu or Buddhist. While evangelicalism remains committed to evangelism, this emerging generation is probably more committed to tolerance, diversity, equality and inclusion.

Young people are different. They value sensitivity, mutual respect for differences and otherness. They are against discrimination on grounds of gender, sexuality, disability and ethnicity. They are likely to be advocates of equality for minorities. This means that targeting, grooming and coercing their peers – this used to be called evangelism in universities – has become a mode of evangelicalism that many Millennials and Gen-Zers now want to keep a safe distance from.

The emerging generation of evangelicals no longer read books from 'approved' publishers that strain and stretch to offer highly tenuous scriptural ground rules for sexual relationships. Nor do they join prayer meetings for supporting missionaries in predominately Muslim countries. In short, most of these emerging evangelicals are different from any who have gone before them.

That is a vast cultural climate change, and most evangelicals I know over the age of 50 are just in denial about it. They work with old weather maps and forecasts and dwell in spiritually insulated, double-glazed, centrally heated bubbles. Many of our Anglican evangelical bishops fall into this category. True, they were never pro-Trump. But customary cultural-climate-change denial, old-style missions, gospel-speak and faith language increasingly sound hollow and inauthentic in an age that values integrity, humility, forms of social and civic service, and kindness.

However, Robert P. Jones has more surprises in his data and findings. Mainline American denominations perform better than their evangelical rivals for the first time in a century. That is, not catching up. They are ahead in the polls. Now, in truth, all parts of the church are in decline – sexuality, sexual abuse scandals, the churches putting reputation and survival before authenticity, truth and integrity are just some of the reasons why emerging generations are not joining churches at all. They remain spiritual but not religious.

However, the churches that do champion the poor, food banks, social justice, climate change, refugees, asylum seekers, equal marriage, equality for women and more are now ahead of evangelicalism in polling for attendance for the first time in almost a century. Some may rejoice at this news. A few may think the trajectory of the inter-ecclesial Cold War (e.g. the CU versus SCM) has seen a reversal.

But this is not what it seems. As Jones points out, cultural climate change is challenging all denominations. The white evangelical voters that put Trump in the White House may now be in steep decline. However, it does not follow that the children of those voters will switch to mainline denominations in large numbers. True, some have, and are undoubtedly attracted by the progressive values and politics these churches exemplify. But the rising seas of cultural change affect all churches, and the signs are not encouraging.

Plutocracy

It is not difficult to see how this all fits with the Church of England, its leadership and the growing discord at the grassroots. The Save the Parish movement begun by Marcus Walker and others is both a symptom and a cause of widespread ecclesial dis-ease with the current administration. A plutocracy is a society ruled and controlled by a handful of people with great wealth and income. The term comes from a Greek portmanteau (wealth + power).

But plutocracy is not a political philosophy so much as a name for a malaise, with the term first coined in English in the 1630s – times of Laudian and Stuart periods of governance, a decade before the English Civil War. The unaccountable and divine right to govern was the issue at stake, over and against the calls for proper democratic structures and political accountability.

Nobody suggests that bishops or diocesan secretaries have significant personal wealth through their ecclesiastical preferment. The modern ecclesial plutocracy is more subtle. Diocesan HQs, Finance Committees, the Church Commissioners and the National Church Institutions have become the new baronial powers, while the ordinary person in the pew and the local parishes have seen their tax demands (i.e. parish share contributions) grow, while accountability and transparency over expenditure have declined.

In short, demands by the centre for more money paired with less democratic accountability will eventually produce movements like Save the Parish. On the ground, its supporters perceive themselves to be giving more and more, and getting less and less. The elites are perceived to be bureaucratic plutocrats, spending money (raised by the people, laity and churches) on speculative projects and visions rather than returning the tax revenues into straightforward public services – which in this case would mean funding clergy and ministry in parishes.

The recent debacle over the Independent Safeguarding Board (ISB) has, for ordinary churchgoers and onlookers, been a sign of plutocratic and elitist leadership. It has been high-handed and anti-democratic: hiring and firing at will, while also asserting the independence of the ISB when it suits, yet treating staff as a subordinate body of subjects with no rights.

The ISB experiment probably cost the Archbishops' Council at least £500,000. Save the Parish would like to point out that the money could have been better spent through greater democratic accountability, proper scrutiny and auditing, and reasonable debate.

LESSON SEVEN: POLITICS AND ECONOMICS

Where does it end? What does the future-scape look like? J. G. Ballard wrote a fine science fiction novel published in 1962 entitled *The Drowned World*. Ballard imagined a dystopian London of the future that has mostly disappeared, submerged by flooding and rising seas. The inability of humanity to control the climate – and our failure to understand how by positive actions and self-limitation, disaster and dystopia could be averted – shape the context for the novel.

In some respects, the churches face the same issues culturally. There is little that churches can do to change the environment around them. They can take some positive action and exercise self-denial, enabling the common good. By self-denial here, I do not mean some narrow Lenten discipline. Rather, self-denial is a moral and spiritual discipline, which may mean, for example, that no matter what churches and church leaders think about equal marriage, they accept the cultural change and adopt it with grace as an act of public service.

To be sure, money, sex and power remain fissiparous and divisive matters for churches at the best of times. But perhaps what churches have failed to grasp in the last 25 years is that, however our internal wrangling has been conducted, social media and 24-hour news coverage mean that the world can tune in and watch anytime without drawing near or joining a congregation or denomination.

Churches preach about justice but won't sign up for the Human Rights Act (1997). Observers notice this.

No Mission Action Plan, Strategy, Governance Review, or bold rebrand can address the deep cultural chasms that have opened up – and continue to multiply – between normal standards and shared values in public life and how the churches act. Reputation management and PR from the churches cannot bridge this gap either. The sea is washing over the very legs of the churches, and our church leaders cannot turn back the tide.

It would be much better to shift to more solid and higher moral ground. Otherwise, we will continue to be bogged down when we want to be congregations and denominations unequivocally favouring equality, transparency, fairness, justice, truthfulness, integrity, humility and accountability. It would mean an end to finding a middle way between sexism and equality. Or 'affirming' people in same-sex relationships or equal marriage, yet not treating them equally.

Church leaders are thought to put the church's reputation before accountability and transparency, But the churches will not be saved by PR agents or some new 'comms strategy'. Only God's mercy and grace can save churches now. Churches urgently need leaders who understand this and respond with humility and humanity.

Summary

A church that tries to evade scrutiny and accountability is only pretending to itself. But the cost of a leadership in cultural-climate-change denial falls on all Christians. Sometimes, the only way to effect change and avert disaster is to change the leadership, especially when it is perceived to be no longer leading in the interests of serving wider society or even the church itself.

We may now need some cultural climate change activists in our churches, taking direct action in an era in which to reform the church is to protest and resist.

Our scriptures and faith emerged from lands and cultures that were constantly at the mercy of climate change, bad harvests, locusts, plagues, disease and wars. We can barely imagine a world in which the very survival of any community or race depended on kind seasons, peaceful living and collaborative labour. Our planet is now out of kilter, and we need church leaders, as never before, to practise fearless care and courageous, prophetic activism in our service to the world.

As the prophet Jeremiah said: 'The harvest is past, the summer is ended, and we are not saved' (Jeremiah 8.20, NRSV). But we are not doomed. Yes, the time is short, the harvest is difficult, and there are few labourers (Matthew 9.37). Churches don't have much time to put things right. They will need to work together. That will require some severe levelling down of existing powers and authorities in the leadership of our churches. The laity, clergy and churches must be levelled up so that local Christian communities become the Arks of Salvation they are called to be. There is always hope, even as the rains fall and the waters continue to rise around us.

For discussion

- What kind of political and economic profile best describes your congregation, and does the congregation reflect the wider community?
- In your opinion, is the increase in secularization the result of increased wealth and social stability, or the result of poverty and political instability? Or is it both?
- Robert Nisbet wrote:

    What are the essential unit ideas of sociology, those which, above any others, give distinctiveness to sociology in its juxtaposition to the other social sciences? There are, I believe, five ... each of these is linked to a conceptual opposite, to be a kind of antithesis ... community-society, authority-power, status-class, sacred-secular, alienation-progress ... they may be regarded as epitomizations of the conflict between tradition and modernism, the old order ... and the new order. (*The Sociological Tradition*, pp. 6–7)

What do you make of Nisbet's antitheses, and where do you find them in your congregation or denomination?

Lesson Eight:
Religious Education

Thirty years ago, most UK polytechnics abandoned their name and identity in exchange for becoming a new university. The government had opened several new universities during the 1960s (e.g. Bath, Sussex) and in addition had created 30 polytechnics in an attempt to ensure working-class communities benefited from the expansion of higher education. Unlike universities, polytechnics were grounded in the cities and boroughs that also supported cognate manufacturing outputs, and therefore specialized in practical degree programmes linked to local industry and the wider economy.

There were notable differences in the approaches to education, training and professions. I can recall some of my peers opting for a four-year degree at a polytechnic, having their place sponsored by an employer, and the degree consisting of a 'sandwich course' that included an academic year spent working in an industry. I went to a university, and read for a degree that could not, in any serious sense, have been said to be explicitly applied or practical.

However, the UK employment and labour market changed rapidly from the 1960s. A combination of globalization and marketization, and the switch from manufacturing and heavy industry to leisure and financial services, contributed to the blurring of the polytechnic–university distinctions. By the early 1990s, the graduate employment market had compacted into a university degree being the best route to a good job.

Furthermore, the rapid cultural shifts stemming from the 1960s onwards had seen the distinctions between working class and middle class dissolve. The 'right to buy' and the collapse of heavy industries in the 1980s had also underlined the cultural and political shifts in education. While this can only be a characterization, polytechnics had tended to serve their local communities and offered more vocational-oriented qualifications, accredited by professional bodies.

The Pedagogy of the Oppressed

The Thatcher government had other reasons to turn polytechnics into 'new universities' or tempt them to do so. Polytechnics were under the control of Local Education Authorities (LEAs), as were many teacher training colleges and colleges of advanced technologies (CATs). The vast majority of these were in urban or inner-city conurbations, under the control of their (usually) left-leaning Labour-controlled councils. Just as in the Greater London Council (GLC), or Liverpool City Council (LCC), with the Labour Party weak and in disarray, LEAs represented front-line resistance to Tory cuts, changes and culture. Labour opposition was led by GLC-HQ, with 'Red Ken' Livingstone on the southerly shores of the River Thames, glowering at the Tory majorities in Parliament.

In 1992 universities were autonomous and funded nationally. There was, therefore, more than a hint of political incentive for removing higher education institutions (HEIs) from LEA control and granting polytechnics university status – replete with new branding, heraldic coats of arms, governing councils and internal infrastructure. Most polytechnics opted for the new identity and apparent freedoms now on offer. Those with reservations or inclined to resist were swept along by the tsunami of educational market forces. In the eyes of most Tory ministers at the time, the post-1992 universities' main role was now to shake off their tiresome left-wing legacies and compete on a level playing field with their older siblings, driven by market-force-led educational consumerism.

However, many educationalists – of all political stripes – will agree that as much as might have been gained by these changes, much was lost. For a start, the rapid decline of 'business-facing' HEIs producing graduates within vocational disciplines and applied research quickly collapsed, much as the industries had in the preceding decade. Furthermore, whatever distinctions that had demarcated 'vocational', 'applied' and 'pure' degrees – as though such labels were ever straightforward – quickly evaporated. Arguably, a distinctive role for higher vocational learning was silently terminated. Whereas teacher training had once been a four-year BEd qualification, with on-the-job learning in schools with distinctive education and formation in an HEI, that was now lost.

Today, almost half of school leavers go to university (or 'uni', as it is usually dubbed). The concept of an HEI delivering training, apprenticeships, sandwich courses and vocational courses has almost entirely disappeared. Where it does exist, it is largely to be found in further education colleges (FECs). Even here, some have obtained taught-degree-awarding powers, or are offering foundation degrees. The polytechnics that were once regularly sniped at by the right-wing press for being hotbeds of unhinged Marxism are no more, and FECs are hardly in any financial or political position to argue for what might remain of the left-wing cause. HEIs and FECs are, for the most part, famished beasts in a land of scarce food and resources, and always fearful of some new famine.

In any case, eggs can't be unscrambled, and the cake cannot be deconstructed to its pre-mixed, unbaked state. Once polytechnics became new universities, the enlarged HEI sibling group has had to adjust to its new intake and size and learn to share out the funding. Research and teaching, as well as student experience and assorted frameworks for establishing excellence, have become the new benchmarks of success. Training and vocations have been left trailing.

Issues for the Church of England

It is on these rather large tectonic plates – unsteady and shifting cultural ground – that theological colleges and training for ministry courses have been sitting for over 30 years. Like the proverbial frog in a boiling kettle, the Church of England has failed to notice the climes of global warming in the educational market sector. It has adapted, to be sure, but with little indication that it understands the environment and culture to which it is subject. But if it is true that there is no such thing as bad weather – only inappropriate or incorrect clothing – we might make some observations at this point.

First, the Church of England's most ancient theological colleges (hereafter referred to as TEIs – theological education institutions) are less than 200 years old. Many denominations did not start to train or educate their clergy in separate institutions until the nineteenth century. In many respects, the mere existence of TEIs was a response to emergent modernity, rapid industrialization and urbanization. Or to denominational schism, and to intra-confessional distinctiveness (catholic, evangelical, etc.). Most of this no longer matters.

Second, the adaptiveness and pragmatism of the Church of England's TEIs began early. Over 60 years ago Southwark Diocese offered one of the first non-residential and part-time courses that afforded a route to ordination, and generally trained older candidates who were to be ordained as auxiliary ministers. The Oxford Ministry Course was developed by Wilfrid Browning (a Canon of Christ Church), to train older candidates part-time with rotational formation using St Stephen's House, Ripon Hall, Cuddesdon College and Wycliffe Hall.

Third, and by the turn of the twenty-first century, more ordination candidates were trained on part-time and part-residential courses than in full-time colleges. With the average age of ordination now north of 40 years of age and many dioceses ordaining more non-stipendiary clergy than full-time paid clergy, the paradigm has continued to evolve. The advent of Fresh Expressions and Pioneer Ministers, together with mixed-mode and blended learning and a brief excursion with Ordained Local Ministry (OLM) training, all point to a particular adeptness.

But there is a meta-question behind these histories and developments. Are TEIs for clergy *training* (i.e. skills, techniques, etc.)? Or are they, following Paulo Freire (*Pedagogy of the Oppressed*), institutions for theological *education* (i.e. questions of belief and praxis, etc.)? Furthermore, apart from collective worship and cohorts of learning, what is the 'formation' that is being offered, and about which many TEIs speak yet few can ever define it? Most Anglicans will use a *via media* here and say 'both'. But before settling on the middle ground, let us consider what is at stake.

Sometimes, vignettes and short conversations are the best way to highlight the issue that needs addressing. I recall a meeting with a former Archbishops' Council Finance Committee Chair a few years ago. Some of us were alarmed at the lack of funding for TEIs, and the growth in 'practical training courses' emerging as the preferred highway route to ordination. In our meeting, the primary goal of ordination training and theological education was explained as evangelism and church growth: 'We don't want to fund ordinands who just want to read books all the time' was how he expressed this viewpoint.

We asked how ministers would be schooled in theological orthodoxy and learning without immersion in two thousand years of Christian writings and doctrine. The Finance Committee Chair appeared to think this was an odd question since he asserted that evangelicals constituted most of the ordinands and the future trajectory of the church, and they knew what they believed. Therefore, their time in a TEI was now to be spent honing practical skills, developing techniques and learning new proficiencies that led to growth. Time in a TEI wasn't for falling into some patristic rabbit hole that debated the nature of Christ over several centuries.

A similar conversation with an archbishop a few years later brought the same insight from a different angle. Over an informal lunch, somewhat to my surprise, the prelate volunteered that they'd recently ordained a few dozen persons who had been 'locally' selected and trained so that they could minister in their locality. The archbishop seemed pleased that the training was relatively short, minimalist and highly cost-effective. Naturally I asked, how would this approach to theological education guard against heresy being preached?

Somewhat stung by the question, it was conceded that a severely curtailed selection and training process would not be able to guide congregations and guard against the newly ordained from flirting with the subtleties of Pelagian or Arian heresies. Otherwise, the job was done – new clergy were ordained. Why was I being so negative about this? Knowing how to respond to this was genuinely challenging, as I have never considered education an inherently cost-effective venture. Education is expensive. But trust me, ignorance and error are far more costly.

Several assumptions lie underneath the approaches of the Finance Committee Chair and the archbishop. I list these in no order since they constitute a cocktail of ingredients, the recipe for which will change according to the perceived needs being addressed.

The first is pragmatism. If it looks as if it works, it must be good. If we can't see results quickly, it will almost certainly be time-consuming and expensive. This is not a helpful fundamental to adhere to when valuing theology, a slow discipline that takes decades for the seed to gestate into good fruit.

Second, it is mechanistic. The Bible itself is treated as a kind of instruction manual or guidebook – there to fix things when they go wrong and to make sure other things work better. A vision for pedagogy founded on such assumptions will provide training and apprenticeships but be suspicious of education.

Third, if the goal of TEIs is training for greater growth and effectiveness, then, of course, education – a pedagogy schooling students in the art of constructive dissent – is unwelcome, as compliance is preferred to critical thinking. Sermons in training-based ecologies school congregations in compliance.

Fourth, sermons that flow from a revolutionary pedagogical model or dissenting educational ecology will challenge and disturb listeners. But hearers will learn to think and engage in the tradition critically. The mechanistic training model won't do that; it would be like trying to argue with the instruction manual.

Training versus Education?

The balance between training and education is based on characterization. TEIs will offer both. That said, the training model will deliver mechanistic instructions and techniques based on its assumptions of revelation and the relationship between divine and human agency. The educational model will see revelation as contested, requiring critical engagement and imagination in interpretation.

Currently, most Church of England bishops support the mechanistic training model. The long-term consequences of such short-termism are yet to be seen, but they are likely to result in a thinner grasp of the richness of faith among congregations and a sense among the laity that they are only being 'equipped' with 'tools and techniques' to achieve certain ends, which are nominated by bishops in strategies, plans and visions.

While teaching that offers techniques that are orientated in mechanistic, pragmatic, restorative, overhauling and expansive aspirations for the faith is to be welcomed, an enormous range of teaching is excluded by such approaches and prioritization. Perhaps this is inevitable, given the pragmatics. After all, many clergy are now ordained after studying for two years, which, in fact, turns out to be around 20 months. They work hard and at considerable cost to their families, partners, supporters and friends. But this is hardly akin to the seven years of education and formation required of a Jesuit novice.

The exclusions that will crop up in sermons and teachings that are the fruit of mechanistic-pragmatic training models would cover, but not be confined to, critical thinking, imagination, wisdom, desert spirituality, analogy and poetry, more profound journeys into contemplative prayer, loyal dissent and authentic revolutionary theologies that seek to resist oppression, confront oppressors, and transform the church with liberationist thinking. (Check out the job advertisements in the *Church Times* and see how many parishes can stress these charisms for their new vicar. For the most part, adverts focus on maintenance and growth – these being the twin concerns of mechanistic-pragmatic training ecologies.)

As someone who has spent many decades in theological training and education, I often wonder how the future might look. Most bishops are university-educated and will also have been to TEIs more rooted in theological education than in the pragmatics of training. Yet I have an uneasy sense that they have turned against the very educational models that formed them and are now over-invested in training, apprenticeship and other models designed to deliver results with stress on training and techniques. At the same time, the bishops have become wary of

LESSON EIGHT: RELIGIOUS EDUCATION

thinkers (they can cause trouble!) and the kind of critical thinking and constructive dissent that comes through authentic pedagogy, including its liberationist expressions.

As one commentator on Paulo Freire's pedagogy has noted,

> There is no such thing as a neutral education process. Education either functions as an instrument which is used to facilitate the integration of generations into the logic of the present system and bring about conformity to it, or it becomes the 'practice of freedom', the means by which men and women deal critically with reality and discover how to participate in the transformation of their world. (Jane Thompson, drawing on Paulo Freire in Peter Mayo, *Gramsci, Freire, and Adult Education: Possibilities for Transformative Action*, p. 5)

There are no bad foods – only bad diets. The answer to this characterization and conundrum is not exclusion or inclusion but rather a deeper reflection on the wisdom of God and its purposes. The art is in the blend. Some problems in the church need mechanistic and pragmatic responses. They are indeed Godly and proper. However, other issues will not be resolved by such solutions, and they will require ministers and theologians of deep learned faith and wisdom to help us think and act. The Church of England cannot afford the loss of either, and it must invest in TEIs, training and education to enable both.

In the Old Testament, both Ezekiel and Jeremiah record a parabolic saying: 'The parents have eaten sour grapes, and the children's teeth are set on edge' (Jeremiah 31.29; Ezekiel 18.2). In a country and culture where few schools teach the basics of Christianity, hymns are seldom sung, our reality is that levels of biblical literacy and Christian knowledge are rapidly depleting. Christian Unions are less propositional at our universities and more inclined to offer fellowship and a certain vibe in worship. A detailed understanding of the Christian faith can no longer be assumed to be present in any tradition before selection for ordination.

Education is critical here, for we cannot presume that the clergy, laity or churches have expressed any sort of wish to be programmed and endlessly reprogrammed. The numbers of churches demanding 'equipping', 'training', 'enabling' and 'setting free' (whatever these terms mean) are few and far between. The risk is that a pedagogy of mechanistic programming will destroy the very heart of what it is to belong to a body of Christian learning. If all sermons are to become a form of coded instruction that reboots the laity and enables them to function better to serve mechanistic means and ends – and along the way, very much treating scripture as one might an instruction manual for a car engine or domestic boiler – then I suspect fewer and fewer will choose church in the future.

Who will want to belong to a congregation prioritizing a pedagogical diet of equipping, training, fixing and productivity? Over and against a culture of rich education and learning immersed and saturated in wisdom, compassion, wonder, awe, inspiration, questions ... and the restless, mindful wrestling with quests that have consumed all Christians throughout the ages yet can never be fully resolved? The choice is stark.

A Way Forward?

There cannot be a better and more urgent time to invest in supporting rich, deep, intensive and extensive Christian theology. But the Church of England faced with this challenge is, if anything, sounding the weak bugle of retreat. It is a pity, as the people are hungry for God and need depth, critical thinking, imagination and stirring. So, if the economics of education are the issue and the driver, what is to be done?

The Church of England has been drifting away from intensive synergies and partnerships with universities for several decades. Departments of theology and religious studies face challenges, including funding and adapting to a new cultural climate. The market-driven interest in religious studies and social scientific approaches to studying religion and ethics has produced stress in the supply–demand chain. Few faculties or departments of theology in the UK are sufficiently nimble and well resourced to adapt to the emerging themes and interests that might draw undergraduates to theology and religious studies as undergraduates. At the same time, universities that were once more intertwined and in symbiotic relationships with local TEIs – including some Bible colleges – have found this to be economically and confessionally challenging.

Furthermore, the discipline of theology and religious studies itself can sit somewhat precariously on shifting cultural tectonic plates. For example, can the Bible, as primary source material, be 'decolonized' as a text? Or, if not, read critically as a text that legitimates oppression, as it plainly has in respect of gender, sexuality, ethnicity and alterity? What would be left of the Old and New Testament if privileged models of hegemonic, oppressive and violent behaviour – national, tribal, etc. – were redacted, or readings that 'decolonized' the text became mandatory? These are real issues for universities.

Indeed, at the time of writing, there were questions of law in the schooling of children in the USA, where one state wrestled with the teachings, stories and testimonies that many today would find offensive, if not traumatic. How are we to offer the scriptures in public life when some of what the Bible condones is either illegal or immoral? Yet they have hardly surfaced on the agenda of most TEIs since the traditions and texts are assumed to be normative and mostly exempt from any hermeneutics of interrogation, let alone suspicion and suspension.

Even setting aside such caveats, few TEIs can match a university department for breadth and depth in theological education and exposure to methods and issues in the study of religion. If we assume that training (i.e. techniques, pragmatics, formation, etc.) remains important for ministerial training – and I do – then 'Houses of Formation' could be developed that are discrete cultures yet also reliant on the excellence of all that a university can offer.

Such Houses of Formation require space and resources for denominational formation, but theological education is heavy lifting provided by the university department. At Oxford and Cambridge, undergraduate theology degrees can be crammed into two years for ordinands or seminarians who already hold a degree in another subject, akin to the Rhodes Scholar model.

Other precedents have been established (e.g. Berkeley Divinity School at Yale), which means an ordinand gets the best of all worlds: great education, training and formation. True, this might be expensive. However, the Church of England's near-200-year experiment in separatism (i.e. its own colleges, courses, etc.) has turned out to be more expensive and, in many aspects, not necessarily superior.

The Church of England now needs an honest conversation about what God might require of education, training and formation for future ministers. Over 30 years ago, Anglo-American theologian Daniel Hardy asked exactly this question of the Church of England.

We are still awaiting an answer. Not what does the church want, nor what can we afford. Instead, what does God require?

For discussion

- If you cannot put a price on education, how much should the church pay to train and remunerate its clergy?

- If the difference between training and education in this lesson is accepted, does your congregation, and do you, want to be educated or trained?
- Peter Schmiechen argues:

> One [method for achieving church growth] is that the techniques can be borrowed from general organizational theory and marketing strategies and have no goal other than meeting people's needs as a way of expanding membership. This opens the door to the great debate over what are legitimate and illegitimate needs for religious communities to meet. While Jesus Christ does in fact meet our heartfelt and deepest needs, in America the gospel too often has become a technique for self-improvement and personal happiness. (*Saving Power*, p. 37; see also Schmiechen, *Christ the Reconciler*)

> If Schmiechen is right, what should the church be about in the twenty-first century?

Lesson Nine:
Sport and Leisure

A sport is not a religion in the same way that Methodism, Presbyterianism, or Catholicism is a religion. But these are not the only kinds of religion. There are secular religions, civil religions ... [as] the institutions of the state generate a civil religion; so, do the institutions of sport. The ancient Olympic games used to be both festivals in honour of the gods and festivals in honour of the state ... going to a stadium is half like going to a political rally, half like going to church. Even today, the Olympics are constructed around high ceremonies, rituals, and symbols. The Olympics are not barebones athletic events, but religion and politics as well. (Michael Novak, *The Joy of Sports*, p. 18)

For many years, scholars have been drawing parallels between sports and religion. Michael Novak's *The Joy of Sports* appeared more than 40 years ago, and was, for its time, one of the most influential treatments of sport as a kind of civil religion in the USA. That is to say, the honouring of values and behaviours that celebrate social affinities are rooted in a kind of 'soft' Deism and have the character of a kind of 'low threshold' and 'common' liturgy. All may observe and participate – through silent reverence, for example – without being specifically active in the ritual. The approach to this lesson, however, takes its basic premise and cue from Michael Novak:

> nearly every writer about sports lapses into watery religious metaphor ... Words like sacred, devotion, faith, ritual, immortality and love figure often in the language of sports. Cries like 'You gotta believe!' and 'life and death' and 'sacrifice' are frequently heard ... sports flow outward into the action of a deep natural impulse that is radically religious: an impulse of freedom, respect for ritual limits, a zest for symbolic meaning, and a longing for perfection. (Michael Novak, *The Joy of Sports*, p. 19)

In what follows, I want to suggest that the popularity of football – including its global appeal – has a bearing on traditional and popular understandings of the secularization thesis. Football is, as Nick Hornby observes, 'a different version of the world' (Nick Hornby, *Fever Pitch*, p. 38). This is one that shapes the behaviours, attitudes and actions of fans and orients them to their environment. Fans, by definition, are *fanatical*; that is, they are obsessively concerned with something. Therefore, in terms of their behaviour, fans do not passively watch matches: they are active participants.

Sport as Faith

The rituals revolving around spectating are fundamental in shaping the football experience. Such rituals (superstitions too!) have been a well-documented phenomenon among sports fans, the most obvious being the ritualistic attendance of matches. (NB: See for example the YouTuber Nieve Petruzziello who goes by the name of 'Stuntpegg'. Her mild, dry, moderately sardonic humour is measured with reverential respect for the liturgical minutiae of football clubs with their specific rituals, and an appreciation of the awe that stadiums and matches inspire that would rival any anthropologist of religion, or for that matter a liturgist smitten by some rite.)

It is still commonplace to speak of football grounds in a rather playful religious manner – the stadium of light comes to mind. Fans of various clubs could claim that their ground was 'hallowed turf'; their stadium a 'temple' or 'cathedral' of football. Of course, we are familiar with explicit religious sentiments and behaviour in football.

One thinks of the annual use and symbolic singing of the hymn 'Abide with Me' at every FA Cup Final. One thinks of the Argentinian player Maradona's 'hand of God' claim when he cheated against England in the 1986 World Cup and pushed the ball past Peter Shilton using his hand. One thinks of Paul Gascoigne's notorious sectarian gesture, pretending to play the flute (pipes) at an Old Firm Derby (i.e. Rangers vs Celtic). Gascoigne, who played for Rangers, pretended to play the flute, celebrating after scoring a goal. The gesture was religiously provocative: a (Protestant) Loyalist symbol from the Orange Order marches in Northern Ireland, in front of the traditionally Catholic Celtic supporters. But each of these brief examples is, as I say, religiously explicit.

That sport and religion often mix is not in doubt. The question is, what *kind* of religion are we talking about? Some of the religion in sport is obvious and explicit. A Muslim football player fasting in Ramadan is newsworthy. Much more commonplace are players making the sign of the cross and looking to the heavens after scoring a goal. But in terms of assessing football, I want to go one stage further and suggest that the actual faith football relates to is not a kind of developed monotheism, or for that matter like any of the established great faiths of the world. Rather, the religion that is implicit in football is a largely unseen type now – at least in the Western world.

I think that if football is any kind of religion, it is of the 'old faiths' that Christianity and other monotheistic traditions largely displaced. By this, I mean the religion of shrines, temples, games, demi-gods and local deities. It is the practice of libations, offerings and little rituals addressing fate and fickleness. Ultimately, we cannot be sure if soccer, or any sport, is religious. But we do know that almost every fan prays that the fickle gods of football will grant their team a slice of luck when Saturday comes. As for the cult of teams that each club spawns, we are not, of course, dealing, literally, with players who claim any kind of divine origin.

But we may be dealing with the many kinds of gods that once populated the ancient world – namely, extraordinary humans who were deified. In Christian tradition, this is not so strange, at least to the Roman Catholics and Orthodox churches, where exceptional individuals are canonized – made a saint. Moreover, these saints joined the 'Communion of Saints', and praying to them was deemed efficacious. There were saints for travel, healing, sport, home – in fact, every area of life.

The Greek and Roman pantheon of gods included mortal-born heroes and heroines elevated to godhood through *apotheosis* (to make divine or to ascribe divine attributes). The demi-gods of football, like the gods of old, and to some extent the Christian saints, do not need to be good, per se. They can, in fact, be quite bad at times and be prone to moods, jealousy, anger and displays of temper. In players like Suarez, Messi, Ronaldo, Cruyff, Salah and Beckham, we have a postmodern pantheon of global, regional and local demi-gods who were 'worshipped' (and if not, at least adored) – perhaps much like their pre-modern legends.

One thinks of *The Sun* newspaper (April 2002), with its front page leading the nation in prayer (with the headline 'Beck Us Pray') that David Beckham's injured foot might be healed before a crucial England match. Readers were greeted with a close-up of Beckham's left foot filling the front page, and readers were invited to lay hands on the image of the foot at noon in a collective act of national prayer.

This is not as provocative as it may at first appear. As Rodney Stark has argued, there are two kinds of religions in the world. The first is older and essentially shrine-based. It was a largely pluralist and consumer-based religious ecology, which involved experiences and rituals including prayer and pilgrimage.

Followers patronized these temples and shrines and were intensely loyal to the gods they followed (e.g., 'I never miss offering a pinch of incense at the shrine of Aphrodite'). These shrines had their 'fans' – literally. And some of those fans became fanatics: real *devotees* to a cult, shrine or god. Many of these shrines and temples had followers who were not averse to travelling to other venues for rituals. The gods who were deemed to be accessible through these rituals and places were appealing precisely because they were quite human in their virtues, faults, passions and practices.

Few of the people who followed these cults – whether of Aphrodite/Venus (love), Perseus (slayer of monsters), Artemis/Diana (hunting), Achilles (hero) or Nike/Victoria (victory), for example – seriously expected these demi-gods to make any interventionist *personal* difference to their lives. Some of these gods were, in any case, simply deified mortals (e.g. kings, queens or warriors who had lived, such as the Roman Emperor Augustus). Others were entirely figures of myth. So, the operant ancient faith worldview, such as it was, therefore depended on fate, luck and destiny as much as it did on any intercession to a deity.

Stark argues that the second kind of religion was more difficult for the ancient world to understand. One God to worship seemed restrictive. Religious pluralism meant cities could have their own local deity to compete with their neighbour's cults, idols, gods and demi-gods, and it was attractive. The monotheistic faiths that emerged and eventually triumphed in the ancient world – Christianity and Judaism, for example – tended to emphasize the omnipotence of God. And as there was only one God, all others were deemed to be either worthless or mere idols.

Football's Forgotten Religious Roots

So, might it be that the actual religious roots of football reach further back in time? To a world quite content with idols, of fate and destiny, of weekly local pilgrimages to hallowed grounds, and to pre-match rituals that might just swing the game against the opposition. Of temples to sport, shrines to players, and fanaticism and support for the gods and demi-gods of football, who seem able to conjure up victory for their team. Of sublimating prayer, passion, grief and hope – and all in the team we still have faith in, despite the results. And who, we pray earnestly, will overcome against all odds and the imminent final whistle. In all this, it is still possible to conjure a world of intercession, hope, gods, demi-gods, victories and triumphs.

Clearly, no one is suggesting that football players are deified. But their heroic status has some distant resonance with deification and canonization. The players' 'cult-like' status – their brand, image, performance – enhances the salvific nature of what they bring to each game, to the team and to the supporters. Indeed, supporters who can become fan(atic)s. Or even become idol-worshippers – for the right calibre of player.

Some of Grace Davie's earliest work on secularization and the persistence of religion focused on Liverpool and attributed much of the religiosity displayed around the club to the city's 'exceptional character'.

She noted how the Kop – where the Liverpool fans stand each game – is a hive of ritualistic activity at Anfield. In previous years at the stadium, there was an area in the Kop known as the 'Boys' Pen', which was designated for the sole use of younger fans. It was penned off from the rest of the Kop and restricted to those who were under 16. It was regarded as a 'safe' area, and being present in this locality was seen as part of the ritual of football fandom. True fans would begin supporting Liverpool and would complete their rite of passage after their sixteenth birthday into the wider Kop. The older fans would stand on the edges and keep a watchful eye on the younger ones, and they would swap magazines, football programmes and autographs.

The refracted religiosity within football – the rituals of attendance, collective singing and chanting and devotion to a club and its stadium – was never more pronounced than at Liverpool in the immediate periods after the Hillsborough disaster. In 1989, 96 Liverpool fans lost their lives (crushed to death in a crowd surge) at an FA Cup semi-final staged at Sheffield Wednesday's ground (Hillsborough), featuring Liverpool against Nottingham Forest. The outpouring of mass public grief led to the Kop end of Anfield being filled with flowers, becoming an enormous memorial shrine. Flowers were left at Hillsborough too. During public mourning, Anfield was treated as more sacred than usual.

Steven Shakeshaft, a photographer for a newspaper, was sent to cover the story. On his arrival at the scene, he commented:

> I felt I was imposing. I had to take photographs and yet I didn't want to. I felt as if I was exploiting the situation ... A Salvation Army band

followed us into the ground, and they grouped around in a circle inside the penalty area and then began playing 'Abide with Me'. It was so spontaneous. We were all in tears. Suddenly, I had a different perspective on the Kop and all those who stand on it. It had become a shrine, their shrine. (Raymond Boyle, 'Football and Religion', p. 45)

The reconstruction of the ground as a shrine, as footballer Ian Taylor noted, was a natural extension of the existing relationships of the club to the fan. Thus, it is not just Anfield in this circumstance, but rather football grounds across Britain that have an almost religious hold on football fans and their families – as those fans will regularly impress their weekend and midweek evening obsessions upon their everyday lives. However, the extent of the public mourning surrounding Hillsborough was unprecedented, attracting worldwide media attention. Much of the press dubbed Anfield the 'Third Cathedral' of Liverpool, and the *Catholic Pictorial* articulated a particularly important metaphor:

> Liverpool became a Three Cathedral City on Hillsborough Sunday. In addition to the Metropolitan and the Anglican, we added the Anfield Cathedral with its two acre liturgically green sanctuary and the Kop altar ... festooned with red and blue 'stoles' and 'albs' which had been sacrificed by the laity in memory of their dearly departed ... the cloisters approaching the Anfield Cathedral were crowded all Sunday, the only sound breaking the silence being the tread of the pilgrim's feet. (*Catholic Pictorial*, 23 April 1989)

The article was littered with evocative religious imagery and sentiment: young men crying, as the seating was covered by the flowers; personal messages left; and even plaster Madonnas. It was the stadium, and not a church, that was selected as the location for this rite. That week at Anfield, double the population of the city would pass through, over a million would file past the Kop; it was, as the press described it, 'The Anfield Pilgrimage', a mass popular religious rite.

The fans have a stake in the stadium. Not only does the white chalk mark the confines of space for the sacred ritual, but the boundaries of the stadium also provide a cathedral for the believer. Ian Taylor noted how he was insistently told by his father and uncle that pitch invasions never happened in their day, as everyone understood that the pitch was *sacred*. It would seem then, that for a lot of fans, there is an inherent belief that their stadium, the green grass of their pitch, is hallowed. We see at Anfield, as Novak describes, that the entire compass of the stadium is marked out as sacred ground for the followers.

For those fans such as Ian Taylor's father, part of their foundation of faith, their belief system, lies in viewing the ground as sacred. The commitment of fans from outside Liverpool, those on the ritual of pilgrimage to Anfield in the wake of Hillsborough, suggests Liverpool may have been a 'Three Cathedral City' long before Hillsborough. For ardent fans, football grounds may be a site of pilgrimage all year round. Some scholars have gone further, suggesting that the attendance at a game, the journey to the ground, a special moment in the match amount to a spiritual pilgrimage which has sacred significance.

Faith in Football

As Novak stated, a sport is not a religion in the same way that Catholicism is a religion. He makes a crucial point in the context of the secularization debate. Viewing the nature of football 'fandom' as implicitly religious shows that religious reality in Britain is probably much more complex than many have considered. Hillsborough highlights that both sport and religion can quite easily work alongside each other, and perhaps even complement each other.

The Hillsborough tragedy made what was normally 'implicit', 'explicit'. In the sublimated spirituality of the Anfield fans, the hidden was uncovered. Not only did the strong cultural identity of Liverpudlians, and the importance of football to their city, make Anfield 'a natural shrine' for the disaster. It also uncovered that, for many, Anfield was a 'natural shrine' akin to a church; it was already a place they considered sacred. Pilgrimage often infers a level of belief, and looking through the lens of implicit religion and understanding the commitments can help uncover the hidden beliefs attached to Anfield. A central tenet in the rubric of their fandom is their belief in the stadium as a 'consecrated place'; a fundamental part of their religious commitment. The lines between football and religion were blurred at Hillsborough. The implicit merged with the explicit; the 'secular' collapsed into the 'sacred'; football banners appeared in churches and religious relics at sporting grounds.

I have been arguing that our society is not more secular and, therefore, less sacred/religious orientated. Rather, 'religion' has become sublimated into the everyday. Some of the clearest evidence for this may lie in football grounds becoming shrines. In some respects, public displays of grief – and treating Anfield as 'sacred' – merely prefigured the public reaction to the death of Diana, Princess of Wales. Yet even before any tragedy, we recall the infamous words of the much-beloved Liverpool manager

Bill Shankly (1913–81): 'Some people believe football is a matter of life and death, I am very disappointed with that attitude. I can assure you it is much, much more important than that' (quoted by James Corbett, *The Observer*, p. 38).

So, in terms of the sublimated spirituality of soccer, we can say with some confidence that 'Abide with Me' is a clear example of an explicit religious sentiment. But we can see here that anthems like 'You'll Never Walk Alone', the everyday rituals of football fans, and what Anfield became after the 1989 Hillsborough disaster, point to something nuanced in the religion–secularization debate. Febrile football fandom might well challenge our classic, conventional understandings of the secularization thesis in twenty-first-century Britain.

For discussion

- Fans, adoration, worship, praise, lament, superstitions, chanting, songs and rituals are all encountered in football support. Can it be helpful to read the apparently secular as quasi-religious?
- Think of other secular institutions that have deep religious roots. Does their spiritual ancestry still 'code' their DNA in the way they are and act (e.g. a hospital)?
- Anthony Giddens wrote:

> The pivotal position of sociology in the reflexivity of modernity comes from its role as the most generalized type of reflection on modern life. The discourse of sociology and the concepts, theories and findings of the other social sciences continually 'circulate in and out' of what it is that they are about. In so doing they reflexively restructure their subject matter, which itself has learned to think sociologically. Modernity is itself deeply and intrinsically sociological. (*The Consequences of Modernity*, p. 14)

> If sublimated spirituality and religion circulates in and out of something like football, where else might we find examples of implicit religion in the modern world?

Lesson Ten: Cultural and Moral Education

Just the other day, I was talking with a wide-ranging group who worked in various vocational professions. Teachers, doctors, paramedics and even a firefighter were present. All agreed that it was relatively easy to work out who they were working for and what they were working against. Doctors work for patients, their practices and the NHS. They work to alleviate pain and suffering. Teachers work for pupils and schools. They work against disruptions to learning and ignorance.

But the issue turned to clergy. Who do they work for, and against what? 'They work for God,' is one opinion that an employment tribunal still might hand down, though that is now changing. Clergy manifestly work for their churches, congregations and parishes. But it is harder to say what they might work against.

Threats and Rewards

These days, the leadership and structures of their denomination pose a significant threat. Churches and denominations live in a kind of legal twilight zone. So, if an allegation is made against a member of the clergy, what happens next?

Ordinary clergy can be 'confined to barracks' for years without an investigation or resolution process. Some charges may be trivial, perhaps a complaint about a pastoral visit, a friendship gone wrong, or other allegation.

Clergy can suddenly discover that 'the bishop and diocese take these allegations very seriously', and then that's it: suspension without an appeal. It could take years to get a hearing. The suspension, imposed by the ecclesiastical authorities, may prohibit going near a school, young people or anyone deemed vulnerable or in pastoral need.

If these conditions are breached there may be a further disciplinary process.

Those on the end of a safeguarding process – whether an allegation or a complaint about how they have handled an allegation against someone else – discover that the complainant, investigator, prosecutor, judge, jury and jailer are all the same people. There is no appeal mechanism and complaints can take years to resolve.

Like sub-post officers, clergy carry ultimate responsibility and maximum culpability without authority or rights. Clergy are relatively cheap labour and can be instantly dismissed. Expendable and exposed, they can be easily bullied by their superiors. The ex-Chair of the Independent Inquiry into Child Sexual Abuse (IICSA), Professor Alexis Jay, specifically listed the 'weaponization of safeguarding' against clergy and laity as a means for some to bully and persecute people, often led by church officers.

In some respects, safeguarding accusations can be seen as medieval witch trials. Officials are unregulated and unaccountable, usually lacking external validation from a reputable secular authority. Safeguarding processes in the Church of England are unregulated by external legislation, and those on trial may find the processes to be abusive and traumatizing. The parallels with the failures of the Post Office over introducing the Horizon accounting system are very striking.

Victims of abuse and those falsely accused face the same problems as the sub-post officers did under its former leadership. The Church of England is quite literally 'a law unto itself'.

I have encountered cases where clergy are told they can claim some legal expenses – usually capped at a few hundred pounds – provided they agree to leave their post before any investigation or complaints procedure. Others are threatened with lengthy complaints procedures that will see them crippled financially by legal fees and are offered a few months' salary to leave quietly with 'an agreed reference'.

With the Church of England unable to fund the clergy it has, the main problem facing the clergy is the very structures and leadership that were meant to care for them.

Moral Paralysis

Things are complicated for the Church of England by its commitment to compromise and finding an accord between incompatible, competing convictions. To make matters worse, its commitment to a middle way is baked into the church. Like the proverbial rabbit caught in the headlights, it doesn't know which way to run.

Some might protest that the Church of England led the way in the abolition of slavery. But after debating it for a couple of centuries it was unable to combine being nice to slave owners and ministering to the slaves in the colonies. Back home, it supported both the slave owners and the abolitionists. The Church of England made sure that those who suffered financial losses as slave owners were compensated, including their clergy and laity. However, the same church leaders also expressed their commitment to emancipation.

The same conflicted moral dilemma can be found in the Church of England's attitudes to polygamy, remarriage of divorcees, women priests and bishops, same-sex relations, how to regard those who commit suicide and even vasectomies. The picture that emerges from each of these debates is consistent. The Church of England considers the moral situation to have been going on for several decades and sometimes a couple of centuries or more. It will rarely reach a definitive conclusion.

If it does eventually make a moral decision, it will find a way to make substantial concessions to those who still dissent, ensure that they are compensated, and be told that their views are honoured and equally valid. This undermines the moral consensus that was reached in the first place.

True wisdom relies on moral courage in making a moral decision and taking moral action. They are not always popular, but expedient solutions that evade moral decisions are a form of fearfulness that does nothing for the cause of truth and justice. They might avoid outright conflict, but rarely build peace and reconciliation. All they do is institutionalize and sacralize division.

Yet church leaders and institutions often struggle to see this and choose the convenience of reasonable compromise, which resolves nothing and merely ensures division and pain are incubated indefinitely.

The Church of England's diminishing moral leadership over the last 50 years is seen today by its silence on recent crises, such as the slaughter in Gaza following the Hamas raids, kidnaps and killings in October 2023. Little has been said by the bishops in the House of Lords on the internecine violence in Sudan or on the ethnic cleansing of ancient Christian Armenian communities in Nagorno-Karabakh.

Yet as late as the 1970s, leading clergy were vocal in condemning US foreign policy in South East Asia. Even an established figure – Archbishop Geoffrey Fisher – could muster an excoriating criticism of the British government during the Suez Crisis. The silence now is deafening.

The Anglican Church has struggled with sex for a long time. The debates over peoples and cultures converting to Christianity that still affirmed polygamy are highly instructive. The Lambeth Conference of 1888 grew out of English colonial opposition to polygamy but had already agreed that 'the wives of polygamists could be admitted to baptism subject to local decision' but not the male party, who could only receive 'Christian instruction'.

As late as the Lambeth Conference of 1920, these issues were referred to as 'missionary problems'. By the time of the Lambeth Conference of 1958, however, things had moved on a bit. Anglican bishops eventually accepted that there might be some serious socio-economic dynamics underpinning polygamy, which were 'bound up with the limitations of opportunities for women in society'. At the 1968 Lambeth Conference, the clauses and resolutions on polygamy were dropped, following pressure from the African bishops, who had talked of the 'great suffering' caused by 'abrupt termination[s]' of polygamous marriages. The Lambeth Conference of 1988 resolved to welcome and receive '[any] polygamist who responds to the Gospel ... [and wishes to be] baptized and confirmed with his believing wives and children'. Overall, Lambeth Conferences have steered clear of polygamy since then.

So, there it is. From 1888 to 1988, the bishops debated polygamy. Eventually, they decided that they could not agree with one another or make the right moral decision, so the subject was quietly dropped from the agenda. Same-sex relations are all set to go the same way, and so there should be nothing more to say after about 2068.

That date would mark a century since 1968, when the Lambeth Conference committed Anglicanism to test the teaching of scripture against the results of emerging scientific and medical research in respect of homosexuality. Bishops were encouraged to have 'pastoral concern' for and 'dialogue with' homosexuals. For the most part, many bishops assume that simply 'listening' constitutes pastoral care; therefore, nothing further needs to be done.

Yet few things are more frustrating to anyone in despair than being 'listened' to by people who are not *hearing* what is being said and, in any case, will not act. Clergy in authority who listen but do not hear, or vice versa, are often unaware of the further trauma this is likely to cause to victims. The culture of the polity is empathetic, mild, reasonable, reactive and pragmatic but also pastorally sluggish and risk-averse. The biblical reasoning, such as it is, will usually consist of sprinkling a selective veneer of scriptures onto some issues, hoping that meaning and relevance will somehow germinate afresh.

The Rise of the Ecclesiocrats

In the meantime, the diocesan CEOs, ever-growing numbers of ecclesiastical bureaucrats and bishops running the Church of England carry on, aided by a cadre of courtiers who run the buffer zones between those pro-this or anti-that.

The crisis of moral reasoning in the Church of England in the twenty-first century cannot guarantee employment, equality or human rights. The public decline of trust vested in church leaders is serious and growing. That means fewer will want to work for leaders and an institution that lacks respect.

Perhaps at this juncture, we inevitably turn to H. R. Niebuhr's classic text, *Christ and Culture*, which offers a fascinating vantage point from which to view how theology, God and the church interacted with 'culture'. Niebuhr's thesis chimed with Ernst Troeltsch's foundational acceptance that Christianity and Western culture are inseparable from each other. This reflects Niebuhr's position that culture cannot be neatly contained in one definition. Niebuhr assessed the theological responses to culture and perceived three mainstream ideologies. First, that culture is entirely neutral to Christ. Second, that culture is hostile to Christ. Third, that culture is solidly based on a natural, rational knowledge of God.

Niebuhr identified several theological responses to how a Christian might engage with culture. First, he sees one dominant response in cultivating distance between Christ and culture, so missionaries require their converts to abandon the customs and institutions of so-called secular, godless or heathen societies. The second proposed the opposite view: a fundamental synergy between Christ and culture exists. Liberal Protestantism has championed such positions.

I do not find it surprising that religion continues to flourish in a capitalist, consumerist and technologically shaped society. True, the forms of religion that now flourish may not be quite what the churches might have hoped for. Spirituality, in all its mellifluous forms, continues to abound.

In contrast, churchgoing – any kind of committed, regular and obligated bonding to an institution – is still under considerable pressure and subject to ongoing challenges in contemporary culture. But it survives and can sometimes flourish.

That said, the challenges posed by contemporary culture are enormous. If we are not captivated by rampant consumerism, our attention is caught in other ways. We are saturated by information and news and have enough gadgets to instantly provide us with all manner of communications and connections. But in so doing, our attention span has been lost. We have somehow lost our capacity to fix our minds on one thing: to gaze with awe or to be still and know. Swept away by current affairs' apparent relevance and power, the breakfast news has become Matins, and the evening news our Compline.

Underneath this technology lurks a deep social suspicion – that we are permanently on the verge of some sort of crucial transformation or secular epiphany that will change how we think, act, behave, react, eat, relate or dress. The moral question is not 'What can this new piece of technology do *for* me, and further enhance my life?', but 'What is this technology doing *to* me as a person and shaping my life inimically?' It is drowned out by the incessant demands of mobile phones, emails and other forms of prompting. Knowledge replaces wisdom; social network sites replace genuine relationships; technology drives out humanity.

One of the most pressing challenges theology and churches face is how to engage with contemporary culture. For many, it seems engagement is a contested and risky affair. Some theological and ecclesiological traditions feel so threatened by the prospect of being overwhelmed or consumed by the task of engagement that they retreat before they have advanced; standing apart from key issues and debates in culture is seen to be the only way of protecting the integrity and identity of the Christian tradition. Others prefer a different strategy, namely one of deep engagement, but in so doing they can find themselves so transformed that they become alienated from their roots. In either form of engagement, a degree of cultural bewilderment seems inevitable.

A Venetian proverb sums up the dilemma: 'The artist swims in the sea, but the critic stands on the shore.' I contend that theology and the churches do not have the luxury of such a choice. To engage with contemporary culture, churches must be critical and artistic. The church must be at home in the sea and on the shore. It needs to immerse itself in the turbulence of the waves (multiple overwhelming cultural tsunamis, as it were) and yet stand apart, retaining a critical distance from the vantage point of the shore (or perhaps some higher ground).

In the present and future, such engagements are going to require church leaders and theologians to be far less reactive, humbler, open to the insights of cultural studies, and alert to how contemporary culture is shaping religion. The more engagements with contemporary culture there are, the more mutations of religion and spirituality will be produced.

With the ever-greater number of mutations comes a greater diversity and less uniformity. Diversification is part of the spirit of the age. It will

LESSON TEN: CULTURAL AND MORAL EDUCATION

be problematic for churches that try to be catholic, universal and uniform in a world of cultural diversity and consumerism. Secularization is but one ingredient in this cocktail.

For discussion

- If moral education no longer comes from churches, scriptures or other faith communities, what are the foundations and sources for moral principles today?
- Can your denomination contribute to faith in public life in a way that doesn't simply privilege your religious beliefs and outlooks? If so, how?
- Charles Taylor said:

Once disenchantment has befallen the world, the sense that God is an indispensable source for our spiritual and moral life migrates. From being the guarantor that good will triumph ... in a world of spirits and meaningful forces, he becomes ... the essential energizer of that ordering power through which we disenchant the world, and turn it to our purposes. (*A Secular Age*, p. 5)

Do you think Taylor is right about disenchantment and migration, and that religion is now a private matter and not for public space?

Governance:
Leadership in Managing Diversity

Dining in an Oxford college some years ago, I was struck by a conversation with the head steward. His role and responsibility were to oversee the seating arrangements, serve food to the guests, and otherwise ensure the smooth running of the many formal dinners scheduled in the college. As a habitual creature of curiosity, I asked him which dinners were the most enjoyable and which were the hardest to manage. His reply provides us with a fascinating window into post-war institutional catering.

He remarked that the most enjoyable dinners – I think he meant easier to cope with – were for alumni who came up to study from the 1950s to the 1970s. He explained that the college dining hall was tiny, serving was much easier if the guests ate the same food. Apart from differentiating between vegetarians and meat eaters, it was straightforward. Even then, he added, the older diners, some of whom had become vegetarians in later life but still could remember wartime rationing, were usually quite happy to leave the meat and fish they might be served with and just eat the vegetables off the same plate.

Alumni from the 1980s to the late 1990s were rather more varied. There were not just vegetarians but also vegans and pescatarians. Still, he said, not that much more difficult.

But at the mention of the alumni dinner for recent graduates, he hardly knew where to begin. Over half the diners had special requests due to food allergies, individual preferences, moral outlooks and life choices. Some pescatarians did not eat shellfish (allergy), some vegans could not eat nuts (allergy), gluten-free diets, food intolerances to dairy products or certain kinds of dairy products, and specified vegetables off-limits (e.g. no onion or garlic), and likewise fruit.

No criticism is intended here at all. I merely record that from the perspective of the head steward, more than 50% of the diners who were twenty-first-century graduates had special diets, which in turn presented an operational headache in this small, confined dining hall. The only way the college had found to manage this with the staffing was to group the diners with specific dietary needs and preferences onto designated tables. This meant that the vegans, pescatarians, those with allergies and those with other special dietary needs were seated together. It is unclear if the individuals dining were aware of how their tables had been arranged, but as pragmatic solutions go, it seemed like a reasonable way forward.

In many respects, this situation is precisely the sort of scenario that might easily crop up at a school governors' 'away day'. Especially if some of those grouped on tables per their dietary requirements discovered they could not sit with their friends. While most would surely understand the challenges the catering staff faces, it is not hard to imagine complaints and protests. Some might even argue that by having their dietary requirements accounted for, they had been inadvertently discriminated against.

Taking personal offences where none were intended is a commonplace problem in the twenty-first century, and institutions treat such situations with great care. Many have discovered late, painfully, and to their significant cost, that even the slightest innocuous comment, misstep or gaffe can easily trigger a storm of anger and a tsunami of social media backlash.

The illustration we have used of trying to negotiate multiple dietary needs and demands serves as a cypher for the complexification of many environments and fora across the developed world. Essentially, there is an expectation that individual choices and needs will be addressed sensitively and equitably. I think that is proper and correct, and such presumptions form the foundation for national and international laws, governance rules and ordinary codes of practice for organizations and institutions.

Equality – of regard for any person, their treatment by others, and opportunity for all – is the primary basis at work here. This accounts for the commonality of anti-discrimination legislation and represents a marked cultural shift in the post-war era. It should be welcomed as a moral, legal, social and political necessity for a fair, open society rooted in equality.

Equality and Diversity in Public and Private Spaces

Of course, it is not as simple as this. I recall a conversation with a recent Oxbridge college graduate who had been heavily involved in the university and college Christian Union. For the university's annual mission, the student managed to secure a free copy of Luke's Gospel for every student in his college. These were to be placed in each pigeon-hole so everybody received a copy.

This well-intended gesture was not without its problems. Some non-Christian students claimed the initiative was invasive of their personal space and beliefs. Others said that this was insensitive, and some claimed that the gesture was targeting and harassing. Most of the Gospels were simply put in the recycling, causing some to protest on ecological grounds that this was a waste of trees, paper and energy costs. Others protested that hundreds of discarded Gospels visibly piled up in a student recycling bin were distressing and might be deemed offensive to minorities (i.e. Christians).

The college Junior Common Room (JCR) was duly summoned to deliberate. It voted – very narrowly – *not* to allow the Gospels to be put in everyone's pigeon-hole. Instead, the CU was invited to leave a stack where, if wanted, students could help themselves.

For the avoidance of doubt, this is not intended to critique Millennials or Gen-Z students. Far from it. I think the college JCR found a sound ethical solution. The vignette is a commentary on the shifting social, moral and cultural ground on which we find ourselves. In talking through the incident with the former student who organized the free Gospels, he said he thought this was an example of how post-Christian and secularized society had become.

I explained that I was less sure. After all, was he not committed to complete equality of opportunity? He was. Was he against discrimination on the grounds of religion, race, gender, sexuality and ability? Likewise, he confirmed he was. So, the question naturally occurred: suppose another religious group, also running a mission or recruitment drive, had done the same thing in the college, such as the Islamic Society (although a discarded Qur'an is religiously offensive to Muslims, as holy books, including the Bible, must not even be put on the floor), or the Jehovah's Witnesses, or a group that others might deem a sect or a cult?

To his credit, he quickly grasped the point. Namely, even he, as a card-carrying and committed evangelical, CU ambassador and advocate, could not square that with privileging his faith over other faith groups. And, although he would still wish to claim that his faith was The Truth (capital Ts), it did not follow that the outlooks and preferences of the CU afforded them a position of privilege over any of the other groups present in the student body.

Food for Thought

Let us return to food at this point. We can agree, I hope, that it would be reasonable to go to a family restaurant and only order and eat vegetarian food. But it would be unreasonable to complain about the other diners eating meat or fish. It is reasonable to request a vegetarian option at a steakhouse, and no good steakhouse would be without such choices on the menu. However, it would be unreasonable and rude to go to a vegetarian restaurant and request a rare-cooked steak.

It would be reasonable to take over a restaurant and manage it as it was, attracting the same custom, especially if it was the only one for miles around. But it is arguably less reasonable for the new manager (please note, not the owner) to refuse to offer simple food that was once on the menu because it troubled the manager's conscience. It would not be reasonable to differentiate between diners, dividing the vegetarians from the meat eaters at tables. Or to exalt those on special diets at the expense of most other customers.

In such situations, there is something to note about permissiveness and the liberty of conscience in a broad society. The needs and requirements of a minority should be respected, honoured and provided for. No one orders a steak in a vegetarian restaurant. Minority views are protected and should be affirmed. However, that does not necessarily make them equal. The will of any minority cannot be determinative for the majority in public space.

Similarly, consider smoking. A minority of people in the UK still like to smoke cigarettes. It is 12.9% at present. Smoking remains lawful. However, restrictions on smoking in enclosed public spaces came into force in 2007. After years of campaigning and public information films, society reached a new mind – by a large majority – on how the personal choices of a few might impinge on the liberty of all.

Smoking in public spaces was no longer a private issue. It is no longer in the gift of a smoker to think through their conscience or manners and then to make their judgement on how nearby non-smokers might react to them lighting up. Smoking in public was deemed to be inherently 'anti-social', and the legislation recognized that one person's liberty to smoke impinged on the well-being of others.

The legislation followed the 2006 Health Act and ensured that smoking was prohibited in enclosed workplaces and virtually all enclosed public spaces. But what about the rights of those who still smoke? Smokers may very well be distressed that cigarette consumption in public has effectively been outlawed and frowned upon.

Yet the reintroduction of smoking zones in restaurants or pubs, in cinemas or on public transport, would impact others. Sometimes, decisions are made for the common good. They overrule individual or collective appeals to personal claims on rights.

So, imagine the Church of England trying to manage the public smoking ban. Perhaps 12.9% of every church hall might be made available for smokers. Or the same percentage of Church of England dioceses reserved for those who are pro-smoking. That would mean having four dioceses and bishops in the Church of England that affirmed smoking. They might go further and perhaps bar non-smokers.

If this sounds a little bit silly, it is. Except it is also serious. There is no middle ground between racism and equality. There is no way of affirming those who might be against people with special needs and disability legislation. It would be a perverse organization that thought the answer to sexism and inclusion in the workplace was to make sure that those who held discriminatory views were equally honoured, must always have full representation, and must also receive certain privileges because theirs is now a minority position.

Discriminatory views on grounds of race, gender and disability complement this reasoning. You may think what you like in private, but you can't necessarily implement such views and practices or air them publicly. So, smokers remain free to light up in their private space. But they are no longer free to share (or inflict) their habit within a broader public sphere. Smokers effectively lost their familiar freedoms – so that wider society could gain equality of experience with fresh air in enclosed shared spaces. There was no feasible compromise.

It was not illiberal to regard 'designated smoking zones' inside restaurants as offensive and anti-social. Nor would it be 'illiberal liberalism' to resist new requests for alternative shared spaces for smokers to compensate for their loss of old customary public places. We would not seek to balance the loss of preference and privilege for smokers by offering them some new public space. We don't say, 'Well, we banned smoking in all pubs, but as reparation, you can now smoke in certain restaurants.'

Implications

The implications for secularization and religion through these analogies are intriguing. Religious authorities, outlooks and public positions are inevitably influential and powerful. They are liminal and subliminal, explicit and implicit. But here, we must distinguish between religion as a public body in which its followers may hold private religious views and positions not necessarily intended for overt public consumption (e.g. divorce). This contrasts with the position any religion might have adopted and be promoting – to influence public discourse and decisions specifically.

What is intriguing about secularization in the Western world, as it affects Christian denominations, is that the churches have become subjects of public discourse rather than shapers, censors or controllers. This means that when churches and church leaders make a statement on human rights, employment law, the rights of workers and personnel, or the resolution of workplace disputes, they are mainly unable to influence public thinking since what they seek to commend to the public is not something that they, as institutions, are themselves practising.

Perhaps in the nineteenth century, the sheer force of power, elitism and privilege that accompanied religion might have meant this simply passed unchallenged. Do as we say, not as we do? However, in the twenty-first century, this undermines religious bodies' identity, integrity and standing. Arguably, this is because many secular spheres of operation have steadily acquired superior and fairer moral frameworks from which to work. Religion can, therefore, find itself *protecting* (i.e. conserving), and even *promoting*, discrimination based on someone's gender or sexuality, and furthermore *privileging* it within churches or faith groups as having some kind of equally valued and valid integrity to those who oppose discrimination on the grounds of sexism or homophobia.

Understandably, the wider world does not want much to do with this. Impartiality, neutrality and compromise are not quite the virtues they appear to be. By engaging in moral reasoning within a secular society, all institutions, including our religious bodies, need to carefully discern what disputes *might* merit a compromise or somehow meet halfway and what issues and conflicts cannot bear such weight and should not, in any case, be expected to.

The difficulty that the governance of many faith communities faces in a secular society is that the leadership (e.g. church leaders) have not been able to discern the recent emergence of a significant dissonance between religious and public values. Consequently, many moral or theological disputes within churches are handled as though they were some kind of intra-community quarrel. For example, where some families, or perhaps a marriage, cannot resolve a row, the way forward might be to find an interim compromise and keep talking. Hopefully, the cause of the original argument and its attendant soreness will diminish and decay over time.

However, some church disputes, like those in families and marriages, are not primarily matters of feeling or perception but rather of principle. We cannot meet halfway on disability, race, ethnicity or the fundamental value of human worth. To even try would be to continue perpetrating injustice and inequality. Appeasement is a short-term fix but rarely a lasting moral or political solution. Maintaining neutrality simply to preserve unity as a matter of expediency will ensure that principles don't matter much, and this will then go on to legitimize oppression.

Secularization debates also run against this background, which is the current failure of church governance. It is becoming increasingly harder for churches to speak in public spaces when their institutions function as private spaces with different and, in the eyes of many, lower public standards of conduct and moral values.

Trustworthiness

That said, and as a rule, the English tend to cherish their institutions fondly. Libraries, museums, the National Trust, local church, memorial hall or post office. All freight an affection and esteem that summon sentiments of collective ownership, belonging and public service. According to one recent poll, the National Health Service was the most trusted. Despite frustrations – queues, waiting lists, etc. - the NHS is loved for its unswerving commitment to universal healthcare (cf https://www.moreincommon.org.uk/our-work/research/the-respect-agenda/ from the University College London Policy Laboratory, September 2023).

It won't surprise many people that central banks, corporations and political parties were at the other end of the league table, scoring low on trust and respect. But what would come as something of a shock was to discover the Church of England and the Post Office hovering precariously in the relegation zone. How did two such venerable institutions find themselves in such a position?

In a word, the problem is governance. Not at the most local level – the local post office or parish. The crisis of trust and confidence is in the institutions' overall governance and senior leadership. Local churches, like local post offices, are usually valued, cherished and well supported by their communities, especially in rural areas. The sub-post officer provides an integral service to the local community. Lose your post office, and people will wistfully opine that the heart has been ripped out of the community. It is the same with closing churches.

The Nolan Principles (i.e. Selflessness, Integrity, Objectivity, Accountability, Openness, Honesty and Leadership in public life) were established by Prime Minister John Major in 1994 to advise on ethical standards of public life.

Similarly, amid considerable scandals in policing, military service, government and churches, the Australian National Audit Office developed an Integrity Framework. The model guides ethical decision-making and helps address risk, fraud and misconduct management. It handles conflicts of interest, vested interests, whistleblowing, corruption and the covering-up of incompetence and misconduct. Its enduring focus is on promoting integrity as a value embedded in work and culture. It promotes the highest standards of independence, honesty, openness, accountability and courage. The higher echelons of Church of England leadership lack anything like an Integrity Framework or Nolan Principles.

All institutions need some level of organization. The family unit is the oldest institution in the world. It will usually be bound together by values, mutual respect, kindred spirit, and the commitment to cherish, care for and love one another despite differences. Institutions quickly unravel when such qualities are absent, and the relationships in bodies such as the Church of England are rarely contractual and instead depend on soft forms of power such as goodwill, voluntary support, trust, careful attention and mindful service.

The Church of England is by no means unique in this plight. Many churches, Christian charities, voluntary organizations and institutions would also fail most of the tests set out by the Integrity Framework. However, what singles out the Church of England here is its power and privilege, which enables it to seek legal exemption from any code of practice that enabled external independent scrutiny. Consequently, whistleblowers are rarely protected, victims re-abused, abuse covered up, and the status quo maintained. The results are inevitable.

As an institution, the Church of England has developed a kind of corporate split personality. On the one hand, its leadership promises to deliver modern corporate step-change management, and has a degree of fluency in such lingua. On the other hand, leaders can operate as inscrutable monarchs might, above any form of accountability or scrutiny, let alone transparency.

The native language of church hierarchy is monarchical. Unsurprisingly, the Church of England's hierarchical structural arrangements function more like a medieval court, thereby only tinkering with cosmetic reform designed to signal modernization and relevance. However, the underlying culture of deference remains intact. The courtiers do not want scrutiny and will not trust democracy. The people might vote for the wrong result. That must be prevented.

As the Church of England continues to lose its status as a national treasure and instead becomes an agency needing membership, support and sustenance, the polity's identity shifts from public service to a model of heavy-duty congregational surcharge. The episcopal and ecclesial leadership find themselves unable to resist the temptations of centralized and bureaucratic oversight, including financial control.

This inevitably develops into a self-secularizing prophecy, in which the charisms of care, kindness and spirituality are steadily squeezed out, to be replaced by growth-related targets and bureaucratic processes piped into the centre.

Paradoxically, this slowly evolving position adopted in the secular realm would depend on demonstrating competence, trust, accountability, transparency and fairness. But this requires management skills and resources that the church presently lacks. In any case, churchgoers do not want this, as these invasive values are perceived to herald from the secular realm and seem inimical to the primary calling and actual identity of the church.

Endpoint

The ultimate end will probably be fragmentation, and, unless checked, it will result in the death of an institution that was once loved and admired by the public. Because of the structures of leadership and uncritical adoption of piecemeal secular organizational and governance templates, the Church of England finds itself caught in a dilemma.

It wants to say it complies with secular-legal standards in areas like HR, safeguarding, data protection and the like. At the same time, however, it does not want to be accountable to a secular regulating authority.

Despite the Glasgow, Jay and Wilkinson Reports severely criticizing the Church of England's record in safeguarding, the Response Group, authorized by the Archbishops' Council to address the concerns, lacks any member with legal or social work qualifications.

One wonders what the public reaction might be if the Archbishops' Council members were to designate an unqualified person to be the headteacher at one of its 4,600 church schools, even though the person lacked subject expertise, a relevant degree or qualification, or teacher training.

The Response Group correlates with this scenario, and the Church of England finds that it no longer commands the trust and respect of the people at large. Its governance has become patchily self-secularized, alienating both insiders and outsiders. A policy of appeasement that avoids making difficult moral decisions risks inflicting paralysis upon itself.

The project to manage the multiplicity of views within the Church of England was challenging in the post-war era, and has deteriorated in the twenty-first century. Secularization in all its forms has posed significant problems and threats to the standing of the churches in the modern world, especially since the post-war era.

Report: From the Counselling Service

Such is the extent of secularization in modern Britain, it may come as a surprise that modern hospitals have religious foundations – St Thomas' or St Bartholomew's come to mind. Halloween seems to have morphed into a secular celebration of light-hearted horror genres, replete with pumpkins. For most, the remembrance of all souls has become quite detached. The religious origins of Oxbridge colleges and other educational establishments are still perhaps easier to grasp, though I do recall interviewing a student for entry into Cambridge some decades ago who had declined Jesus, Christ's, Trinity and other colleges because of their religious names, but had chosen Emmanuel. I truly wish this were an urban myth; but it isn't.

So, when teaching the sociology of contemporary religion, and trying to help students come to terms with normative practices, institutions and organizations in everyday life, many are surprised to discover the religious origins and purpose in football clubs such as Liverpool, Everton, Manchester City, Rangers, Celtic and more. It comes as more of a surprise to discover that the DNA of basketball was rooted in the late nineteenth century, with clergy and well-meaning Christians developing a (largely) non-contact sport for small church halls, to keep wayward inner-city youths exercised, absorbed, healthy and off the streets.

Decoding the Secular

Contemporary celebrations of Christmas are similar, and it is undoubtedly the case that the modern Santa Claus was contrived by New York High Anglicans engaging in some intentional social engineering. The Service of Nine Lessons and Carols – another Anglican invention – was Eric Milner-White's answer to the appalling lack of Christian knowledge he had encountered among working-class soldiers during the Great

War. His Service of Nine Lessons and Carols was designed to tell the Christian story from Genesis to Revelation using rousing English folk melodies, hearty carols and no sermon. The service was also designed to last less than an hour. Long before Alpha courses kicked in, enterprising clergy reckoned that an hour of scripture and song could get the gospel message across. I concur.

The modern problem page, to some extent, originated from religious roots and social, moral and spiritual concerns. John Dunton was a 32-year-old printer and bookseller. It was during the winter of 1691, while out walking in the fields of Lambeth, that he sought to wrestle with his conscience. He was, by his admission, contemplating an extra-marital affair.

For Dunton the matter remained one of torment, but the walk gave birth to an idea. Suppose he were to publish the nature of his anguish and its consequences, using a letter with a pseudonym, and seek public advice on the right course of action. The device of audience participation in a moral dilemma was born and first appeared on 10 March 1691, in *The Athenian Gazette*. (The modern successor to such approaches in newspapers today often blends expert advisors with members of the public contributing insights and suggestions.)

John Dunton (1659–1733) founded The Athenian Society to publish *The Athenian Mercury*, the first major popular periodical and first miscellaneous periodical in England. In 1693, for four weeks, the Athenian Society also published *The Ladies' Mercury*, which was the first periodical specifically designed for women readers. Dunton hardly lacked for religious interlocutors in his background. He could trace his roots back through several generations of clergy, and he himself was related by marriage (through his sister) to Samuel Wesley, the father of John and Charles.

Dunton was no progressive post-Christian liberal. The established hierarchical order of religion and morality remained unchallenged. But even in the later seventeenth century, the ground was shifting. Theatre, opera, publications and entertainment both reinforced and challenged prevailing social, moral and intellectual norms. In an age of emergent Deism, few expected God to act as some kind of school headmaster or the clergy as God's prefects to issue censorship and retribution. Increasingly, the moral judgement and social pressure of society played an important role in the ordering of society. The significance of Dunton's initiative should not be underestimated since this is the first record – in print, at least – we have of experts and members of the public commenting on personal social and moral issues that vexed individuals.

From the outset, we encounter the light-touch counsel and occasional tongue-in-cheek chastening we find from agony aunts today. For example, one of Dunton's correspondents wanted to know if it was permissible to pray to God that his wife might die – they had been separated for many years – in order that he might remarry. In the seventeenth century, 'till death us do part' meant what it said. The *Athenian* responded by stating that if his 'wife were fit for heaven, then she is fit for you', before adding that it would be 'handsomer to submit to God's will and wait with patience', before signing off with the mildly chiding suggestion that a better prayer might be to ask God to convert the parties into more lovable individuals.

Problem Pages as Barometers of Social Change

Robin Kent's illuminating study of agony aunts, *Aunt Agony Advises: Problem Pages Through the Ages*, provides us with an engaging study of the problem page as a kind of barometer and guide to the social and moral predilections and dilemmas that absorbed individuals and wider society. Although these are not our issues so much, they still relate to us as arenas of conduct and conscience that need settlement. Robin Kent correctly identifies courtship, marriage and divorce as key issues. But also surfacing are issues of etiquette, personal medical issues, family dynamics and social stigmatization. Widows, spinsters and 'ruined maids' frequently crop up as correspondents with their issues. Religion, spirituality and contemporary morality also feature strongly.

Reading the correspondence and counsel of problem pages from 300 years ago gives us an illuminating insight into the vexing issues that individuals wrestled with then. Of course, these have changed over time. As their popularity spread to mainstream publications, we find individual correspondents – and the replies – describing the emerging moral and social landscape of their time.

The latter half of the twentieth century sees many agony aunts in national newspapers and magazines frequently grappling with sexuality. For the most part, the problem pages handle the anguish, torment, confusion and desires articulated with a fine blend of compassion, care, empathy and emotional intelligence, along with practical counsel and pragmatic suggestions. Yet even now, problem pages from just 50 years ago are a stark reminder of the social, personal and moral issues that individuals wrestle with.

To study early editions of *Gay News* is to enter a world of stigmatization, marginalization, resilience, hope and determination. It is interesting to read how the Church of England's early official reports on human sexuality had been received by the subjects of debate. Archbishop Robert Runcie commented that the report provides 'food for thought', and *Gay News* notes him speaking out publicly for 'compassion'.

The letters pages from *Gay News* provide us with a model of strong, gentle, considered, compassionate and caring correspondence. Moreover, in many respects, we are offered a mirror to what the agony aunts offer through their counsel.

Problem pages are a virtual 'confessional box' in which the reader can overhear what is being poured out and eavesdrop on what the remedy might be. Some confessions prompt chiding and censure. But many evoke compassion, empathy and caring – the kind one might reasonably expect from a therapist or counsellor. Much of the advice is non-judgemental and returns agency and confidence to the correspondent. Indeed, what is striking about so many agony aunts is their capacity to range over moral, social and personal issues, yet without lapsing into some patronizing lecture.

The terrain of presenting issues that agony aunts engage with is entirely cognisant with the open and ambivalent texture of pastoral counselling and conversation. Feelings of shame, guilt, inadequacy, grief, anger, confusion, resentment, bitterness and more besides are engaged with in a manner that is undoubtedly receptive, succinct, yet belies the wisdom offered. If problem pages are, effectively, a confessional, the respondent speaks over the head of the correspondent to the readership. We are offered a pulpit of intimacy; an altar of transformational communion; an exchange of peace; conditional or fulsome absolution for the sin and shame that seems to cling so closely, yet, received, heard and resolved can lead to healing and liberation.

Third, and as John Hardy reflects, even our ordinary weather-related talk takes the form of sublimated spirituality, and hints at the calming liturgical-like chant of the shipping forecast on BBC Radio 4. It *soothes* us. Agony aunts seem adept at comforting the afflicted, and occasionally afflicting the comfortable – the smug and self-righteous. Here, I am very struck by Emma Percy's readings of the transformations captured in the *Queer Eye* TV series – kindness, care, attentive listening and discernment in the detail matter to those who are bound by social, moral religious constraints that oppress.

Can it really be the case that agony aunts offer us something that can be ascribed to implicit religion? I think so, since their counsel constitutes a form of pastoral chaplaincy in public space – be that the family home, workplace, bedroom or other arena. I think of the *Doonesbury* cartoon (by Trudeau, published in June 1993), where a soldier wounded in hospital after the first Gulf War and struggling with PTSD unburdens himself to another officer who is clearly a skilled listener and reflector. The wounded soldier asks if the officer is a chaplain? The confidant replies that he is not, but instead should be regarded as the 'Morale Officer' for those recovering from the trauma of war, and those made to witness this in their roles.

Implicit Religion in a Secular World

Concepts such as morale, counsel, kindness and compassion may seem like common fare for the caring professions, but I hold them to have an intrinsic religious quality that offers an entirely different perspective on the 'priesthood of all believers'. In the problem pages, we frequently find an almost ritualistic confession-counsel-absolution sequencing, only lacking the gospel punchline 'go, and sin no more'. Yet what comes through the office of an agony aunt is the delicate and reticulate blend of the feminine, maternal, caring, listening, compassion, kindness and counsel. Agony aunts are there to guide us – spiritually, morally, emotionally and pastorally – and they do so with an attentiveness that lends itself to an interpretative framework that would not be unfamiliar to those engaged in the field of implicit religion.

Of course, I recognize that we are making use of a relatively rare sociological *lens* – that of implicit religion (a term coined and defined by the late Edward Bailey, 1935–2015) – and analyse as Bailey might have done. Bailey was both a theologian and sociologist, and as an Anglican clergyman and academic had an additional platform from which to assess everyday life. Implicit religion, as a 'lens' for reading current patterns of social behaviour, simply refers to people's commitments – whether they take a religious or secular form.

I use the term 'lens' here with some care, as implicit religion is not a methodology per se. In common with many other kinds of sociological outlooks, implicit religion is a 'take'; a way of viewing the apparently ordinary and familiar. Implicit religion is not like the lens of folk religion, which looks at specific acts of communal and individual spirituality that are largely outside the control of mainstream religious activity. Specialists in the study of folk religion usually focus on beliefs and practices that survive the imposition of official religious monopolies.

Implicit religion is an approach that is neither civil nor folk in broad outlook. It is, rather, an intentional focus on ordinary everyday activity that may appear, at first sight, to have no element of spirituality or religion to it whatsoever. Moreover, the participants may have no explicit idea that what they are doing can be read and understood as 'religious'. So, their participation is often unconscious. Or, as Edward Bailey maintained, a matter of implicit religion.

What then, of implicit religion as a lens for understanding agony aunts? Something that is implicit lends itself to eventual surfacing and being made explicit. Following Bailey, I hold that the lens of implicit religion is essentially bifocal in character. It allows through an oeuvre or single aperture, to both focus on something that lies in the foreground and yet also see something else that lies at a far greater distance.

In Bailey's case, the bifocal lens of implicit religion permitted him to focus on immediate, ordinary everyday human activity. And the more distant subject was, as ever, the realization that we could not escape the horizon of secularization. Bailey's bifocal lens brought the two together and placed them in a single framework (or lens) for discussion. This approach 'opens up the possibility of discovering the sacred within what might otherwise be dismissed as profane, and of finding an experience of the holy, within an apparently irreligious realm' (*Implicit Religion in Contemporary Society*, p. 3). Bailey argued that the lens of implicit religion permitted several insights to come together as (what he termed) 'integrating foci' – the possibility of seeing 'intensive concerns with extensive effects', for example.

Even more fruitfully, perhaps, concepts of implicit religion can act as a counterbalance towards the tendency to automatically equate 'religion' with specialized institutions, articulated beliefs and specific religious behaviour. Above all, the lens of implicit religion allows us to read aspects of contemporary culture and conduct for nascent elements of religiosity within what, to the more casual observer, might conventionally be seen as a normative secular sphere. As Timothy Jenkins' work has shown, the implicit religion lens can illuminate the simplest things in our communities. His description and analysis of the mildly chaotic jollity of a community-led 'Whit Walk' in a suburb of Bristol is a perfect example of the implicit religion lens bringing a curious social phenomenon into sharper focus.

Summary

Sociologists continue to narrate the fate of religion in the developed world as one of believing without belonging; spiritual but not religious; of consumption rather than obligation. Whether or not this trajectory continues some stable course, any portrait of religion receding in the twenty-first century has to reckon upon what is surfaced when the tide goes out. It is at these points that the new secular confessor-pardoner-pastors – as many agony aunts have now inhabited such roles – become visible reminders of the resilience of religion. Our age is not irreligious. All the evidence points to our constant and enduring quests.

Agony aunts engage in the untidy and broken lives of others. They deal with the tears, aches and broken points of human existence, including shame, self-loathing, suicidal thoughts, heartbreak, bereavement, aching loneliness, feelings of inadequacy, and a panoply of fears. Agony aunts respond to those who struggle with the confusion of who they are and what they are becoming, in terms of identity, sexuality, gender – so many uncertainties and unknowns. In a world saturated with information and awash with communication, these open confessionals soothe, succour and support those who are feeling bereft, confused and exposed.

Happily, there is a parable to take note of. In 1935, a young woman wrote a letter to *Nursery World* magazine, expressing her sense of isolation and loneliness. Women from all over the country experiencing similar frustrations wrote back. To create an outlet for their plentiful ideas and opinions they started a private magazine – *The Cooperative Correspondence Club*. The deep friendships formed through its pages ensured the magazine continued until 1990, 55 years after the first issue was published. Jenna Bailey's *Can Any Mother Help?* captures the essence of these letters which testify to the value of shared counsel, wisdom and compassion.

Likewise, the modus operandi of agony aunts, and their pastoral homilies through their problem pages, resonate with implicit religion: 'intensive concerns with extensive effects' (*Implicit Religion in Contemporary Society*, p. 6). Problem pages represent a late-modern development that, like hospitals and other institutions, suggest a more hopeful outlook for faith. Secularization theses and ideological secularism assume society is becoming less religious as it develops. However, those who choose to read and interpret the world through the oeuvre of implicit religion will find religion in unexpected places. Granted, it may be outside the domain of formal and official religion and in the sphere of the informal and operant.

Yet, as hospitals undoubtedly know, basketball testifies and problem pages and agony aunts witness, faith and hope represent an embedded ingredient within our 'social mix' – from the outset. One can no more separate out religion from society than remove the egg from a cake. It is always baked in … even if one can no longer taste and see it. Trust me on this. Religion, change, faith, forgiveness, love, redemption and the hope of God are ever-present. This is how we live.

Term Ends:
Closing Assembly and Farewells

We will need to rethink the relationship between religion and the secular in the future. Traditional approaches to religion and the secular appear increasingly unfit for purpose. The categories 'religion' and 'secular' have been problematized at a time when fundamentalisms of several kinds have gained in strength and prominent international scholars have questioned previously prevalent secularization theses. Responding to these challenges requires a concentrated rethinking of what religion and the secular are involved in and their scope and prospects.

The terminology is also not what it was. Oceans of spirituality flow through secularized societies every minute of the day. We can see this very clearly in the emerging 'soft religions', which focus on personal and collective support that is 'spiritually freighted'. Mindfulness is one example, but many forms of yoga, therapies and fitness-related practices now incorporate spiritual practices and beliefs.

At the same time, affiliation and obeisance to religious groups and their structures, powers and authorities continue to become more attenuated. This is often described as a 'consumerist' approach to religion. If it is, the public buys much less of it and shops around a lot more. This leaves religious organizations with a problem regarding the growing gaps between believing and belonging. As we noted earlier, a 'committed churchgoer' used to attend church twice on Sundays, observe high and holy days, and perhaps belong to a midweek Bible class.

Most 'committed churchgoers' in twenty-first-century secular society will not follow this pattern. They're unlikely to be at church on a Sunday more than once. They're unlikely to manage high or holy days that don't fall on Sundays. They're unlikely to be part of a midweek Bible class. The self-secularization of the churches means that what spare time people might have for church activities will be committees, regulatory obligations, church business, fundraising and maintenance.

Performatively, 'committed' declined in value and is pegged to 'regular'. It could mean three out of four Sundays a month. But it is likely to mean less than that. Churches have attempted to address this cultural drift or cover it up by moving high and holy days to Sundays. Epiphany (6 January) will be celebrated on its nearest Sunday. Many other festivals have followed suit.

At the same time, Remembrance (11 November) has bucked the trend, and is kept whatever day it falls on. Remembrance Sunday continues, too, and the fact that both are now such visible sacred moments of silence, spiritual reflection and recollection suggests that secularization is patchy at best. We note with interest that Harvest Festival, Mothering Sunday, Remembrance Services, Christmas and Easter continue to enjoy widespread public support.

That said, the traditional sites for the secularization versus religion debates are undergoing profound change because of new technologies (e.g. AI, intelligent robots, genomics, social media), the human impact on the environment (e.g. climate change), globalization (e.g. refugees) and so on.

The religious dimensions linked to these developments are complex and intertwined with ethical concerns. The rise of Muslim extremism in Europe, North Africa, the Middle East, South Asia and South East Asia utilizing new technology grounded in religious fundamentalism has generated a host of issues in counter-terrorism ethics regarding freedom of expression on social media. Religious institutions are heavily involved in the provision of welfare services for the aged, infirm and impoverished (including refugees).

Accordingly, many of the de facto but ethically contested responses (e.g. regarding the extent of obligations and the possibility of corruption of processes) are being made by institutions operating within a religious framework. Traditional religious conceptions of 'stewardship' in relation to the environment relate in multiple ways to issues in climate ethics. The consequences for institutional and public life, society and across national boundaries are significant, not least in security, climate change welfare provision and, relatedly, the response to new technologies. The future looks complicated with the ethical challenges of faith communities and religious institutions.

One of Jesus' best-known parables (Matthew 7.24–27) is conventionally referred to as 'the house built on the rock', in contrast to the one erected on the sand. The story of the two buildings, or builders, is a word to the wise. Indeed, Jesus' parable is the archetypal cautionary tale, and seems such a prominent piece of common sense the points barely seem worth making. Impressive buildings can be quickly erected and may be visibly appealing. However, it is the invisible and functional foundations that will determine the longevity of the building. Jesus has similar things to say about seeds, roots and soil types in the Gospels.

Readers will have their own views as to whether society is in the grip of secularization and what that might mean. I think we must concede that the churches and denominations, as organizations, are in serious trouble. But that doesn't mean accepting fatalism. At the same time, the so-called secular society seems perfectly friendly and accommodating towards spirituality and certain kinds of common rituals (as noted above).

Whatever zealous proponents of secularization imagined the future to be, it seems that it is not going to be a world of technology, materialism and empiricism that eliminates God. The twenty-first century, for all its advances in the sciences and technologies, remains absorbed by the capacity of spirituality and religion to provide comfort and enchantment in the world.

The threats to religion will come from other quarters. For example, there may be civil, political and economic strife in societies that trigger revolutions or internecine civil wars, that turn against religion and faith communities. While this has happened before, the risks appear now to be markedly higher than they were at the end of the twentieth century. More broadly, the grammar of dissent and protest seems to be returning to the levels witnessed in the 1960s.

At this point in time, the churches are not on solid foundations; nor are they sure-footed. Money, sex and power – that unholiest of trinities – afflict all mainstream denominations. Consider the history, data and internecine ecclesial wars, and try to name any exceptions. In my view:

1 No churches have escaped internal wranglings and unease over their lack of money and its unequal distribution, the method of 'taxing' congregations, and how the revenues are spent.
2 No churches have so far managed to navigate unscathed same-sex relations, scandals on clergy and sexual abuse, divorce and remarriage or arguments and issues over gender.
3 No churches have found ways to balance democracy, leadership, management and compliance without getting caught up in plutocracy, despotism or abusive forms of theocracy.

One might say that the most significant regime change in ecclesiology is the East–West Schism or the Reformation. But in truth, smaller versions of these global ruptures have occurred in every generation. Some result in permanent rifts and then further extended fragmentation (e.g. sects inadvertently derivative of denominations), while others are managed by loosening ties while retaining weaker centrally controlled identities. Only very occasionally are rifts healed and relations restored (e.g. Scottish Presbyterians).

However, the cultural ground in which the foundations of mainline denominations sit is no longer a stable commodity. The emergence of meritocracy, less deference, mass mobilization, greater individualism and consumerism in expressions and preferences all conspire to render the ground of being for the church unstable and shifting. Congregations still sing that the 'church is one foundation', but the ground upon which it is founded is one of increasing instability.

Peter Turchin explains how regimes rise and fall, and what it is about forms of control and the exercise of power that makes some types of governance especially susceptible to implosion or overthrow. It is Turchin who also coined the term 'cliodynamics' – Clio, the muse of history in Greek mythology, and dynamics simply the study of how and why change takes place over the generations. Using modelling theories, a cliodynamic approach can predict expansion and retraction in economies, state collapse or implosion, social discontent and even civil wars. It is not a perfect science, but it often goes some way towards explaining how and why institutions and societies collapse.

So, what would a cliodynamics approach make of the Church of England at this point? Several observations are immediately apparent and will create the conditions for instability:

1 Major shifts away from more open electoral systems to ones that are more closed, authoritarian and have managed control systems produce boredom and detachment, festering resentment. They may result in speculative conspiracy theories (e.g. we know where all the money goes …).
2 Elitism, whether quasi-monarchical or some ontologized managerialism, will result in a larger critical mass resenting hierarchies and their powers of rule and decision-making. A lack of accountability, transparency, integrity and humility will also produce calls for regime change.
3 Loss or rapid erosion of devolved local powers, assertions of control (e.g. adopt the strategic vision) and penalties for daring to dissent will create a groundswell for secession, in which the exercise of despotic power will only produce tensions between central control mechanisms and those meant to comply.

4 The collapse of the central governance, inability to manage external complexities and challenges, and inability to fund, manage and resource internal systems of order and control will tend to question the capacity of the ruling elite to hold authority, power and any ability to govern.

The churches are self-secularizing faster than ever, and the adoption of business models, investment in more bureaucracy, and macro-organization look set to drive out more people than they bring in. The results are not hard to predict. But those driving the changes deny the trajectory. Like Orwell's Ministry of Truth in *1984*, communications and assertions no longer correspond to reality.

Secularization is alive and well, but it is not terminal for faith. So, there are farewells here. Everything that has been discussed and debated will be reappearing on the syllabus. Yet, there will be adjustments as we return to the curriculum. What is of more concern now is the serious disenchantment that has set in in the churches and continues to swell. Real questions and issues are being raised about the trajectory of the church from those in the pews. However, the responses to these from the leadership are increasingly evasive and coy.

The writing is on the wall. Church of England attendance figures are 20% down since the pandemic (one in five did not return), and 29% down since 2015 (according to the CofE's own statistics for mission). The 2022 financial statistics record similar alarming levels of decline. The number of regular givers has dropped from almost 540,000 (2016) to just over 400,000 in 2024. Parish contributions have fallen by 10%. Vocations to ordained ministry have collapsed by around 40%, down from 650 (projected) to 350. Most dioceses have some structural deficit, with 35 of the 42 running at a loss. There is significant disenchantment. This age has morphed, in the view of Eugene McCarraher, into one where capitalism has become the new religion of modernity, and seemingly offers the best hope of social salvation and personal transformation (McCarraher, *The Enchantments of Mammon*). If the deepest longings of humanity are no longer being met by searing spiritual insight, deep theological wisdom, and prescient social prophecy, we are indeed entering the later stages of church life (Halík, *The Afternoon of Christianity*), and the dusk of Christian faith, not some new dawn.

Vocations for ordained ministry are a particular concern. In 2034 the Church of England will mark its 500th birthday. By then the number of stipendiary clergy in the Church of England will have fallen to just over 5,000. That represents around half the number when I was ordained in

1990. It is also more than 2,000 fewer than the recent target set under the much-heralded Renewal and Reform, the strategy document published with much fanfare by the Archbishops' Council in 2015. Not a single target it set has been met over the decade since publication, and many of the issues it sought to tackle have only deteriorated further and faster.

For example, the number of retired clergy has increased by 36% since 2000, and the number of stipendiary clergy has decreased by 22% in the same period. More clergy are now retiring than being ordained, and that trend is set to continue for the foreseeable future. The working conditions for clergy have noticeably diminished in the twenty-first century. Clergy have few employment rights and meagre pensions to look forward to. But long before that, they can be dismissed at the whim of their bishop, who can simply decide not to issue a licence enabling any future ministry. Under such conditions, ordained ministry has become unstable, unsafe and, if trying to raise a family on only a stipend, unworkable. Most dioceses now run large recurring financial deficits, but the bishops just pass the costs of the cuts on to the clergy and congregations. In all of this, the Church of England will claim it is fully compliant with the 1998 Human Rights Act, while operating a form of indentured employment. Despite this, bishops remain unaccountable to any HR process or scrutiny of their governance, which only fuels more disenchantment.

As with any regime, the church now finds itself on the brink. Its members and congregations must increasingly choose between unwavering loyalty and compliance with the authorities. Or engaging in difficult questions and actions of dissent that might involve them in expressing a mind that sees and seeks better alternatives. There are winds of change.

In conclusion, however, I want to draw our attention to the blessing of exile. Yes, you read that right. Exile can be a blessing. We might say that one can summarize the Old Testament in a single word: 'Wait!' Just as the New Testament bears summary in one word as well: 'Go!' The church, like the children of Israel, cannot see the work of God in the refining fires of exile, and the long, long treks in the wilderness. But it is in displacement and discomfort that the people of God recover their identity, core and vocation. In the New Testament, the church is charged with being expelled into the world, not taking the world into itself. The church is not here to recruit. It exists, after Christ, to be self-emptying.

Exile is a time of preparation, re-ordering, purging and reform. As Daniel and the prophets knew, there is no going home to the Promised Land until the lessons have been learned. The most important of which is to reckon with how and why God allowed the people of God to be displaced. This is a matter of faithful integrity. When the people of God discover why they have been exiled and what God wants to teach them through this experience and this time, the blessings can begin to be discerned. The church is in exile. That is a state of blessing, not curse. God has things to accomplish and teach in this era we are now in. So, let us learn how we are to be blessed by being stripped of our powers and positions in this secular age, and once we learn to accept the blessing of deprivation and dislocation, only then might we discover that less is more. God meets us in exile. God will not release us from it until we have learnt our lesson. That lesson will be a blessing. We have only to learn what it is to embrace it. Until then, this exile still has more to teach us all.

Future Directions:
what3words? Go, Make, Disciples

You can navigate and find yourself anywhere in the world by using just three words. Feed your location into a search engine, and you'll be assigned a random three-word location code. Currently, mine is 'class, lunch and march'. Yet the what3words app for locating and navigating the church nowadays seems to be 'go, make, disciples'. My question for the churches is, 'How *faithful* is this as a direction?'

The genesis of these lesson notes has gestated over many years, and I owe readers some stories to explain my concerns. Most churches and denominations simply do not understand what kinds of cultures they are immersed in, let alone the tides of secularization that might be flowing through the attitudes of the communities, societies and contexts in which individuals and groups are set. Because Christian groups typically regard themselves as wholly other and distinct – apart and aloof from the world, and even a 'law unto themselves' – they struggle to see how their proposals and remedies in relation to the vexing issues they think they are experiencing and facing are, in fact, misconceived. Trying to impose an idealistic and aspirational vision, yet with an ultimately quite thin theological or spiritual framework to contain pressing problems, will rarely work.

The Cost of Discipleship (has gone up again)

It is a fact that nearly all the top-down-hierarchy clergy-led directives, sermons, strategies and visions for more lay leadership are quite new, dating only from the late nineteenth, twentieth and twenty-first centuries. Within the time frame of modernity, that clearly indicates that the emphasis on lay ministry is an inchoate response to the broad experience churches have of secularization. Typically, the quasi-spiritual-visionary rhetoric will sound authentically biblical. Thus, 'every-member ministry', 'the ministry of the whole baptized people of God', 'everyone has a vocation and calling, and so everyone is a minister', will be rolled out into parishes, unfiltered, as though it is obvious that the scriptures themselves teach this.

They do not. Not every follower of Jesus is, or ever was, a disciple. Many laity do *not* have a vocation or calling. But they are happy to help out at certain times with certain things if asked (nicely). But they are generally unresponsive to attempts at spiritual blackmail which suggest that simply by virtue of being part of a church, they have a mandatory vocation, calling and ministry, and must discover what that is, have it discerned and affirmed, offer it back to the clergy, who will then put their urgent tasks, roles, jobs, demands and obligations on a more formal footing.

I am not saying that the clergy must do all the work and the laity need do nothing. Nor am I saying that laity cannot have a ministry. Many do so, and the world and church are all the richer for and blessed by such. But even if any layperson does discern and exercise a ministry, they are free to lay it aside at any point and not obliged to resume it. There is no contract that binds them to a role, and no means of compulsion when they relinquish it.

Currently in the Church of England, one by-product of secularization is the demands of legal compliance falling on churches – insurance, safeguarding, health and safety, maintenance, money, fundraising, trustee duties – which now makes it hard to find *anyone* to be a churchwarden. Fifty years ago, vacancies for being churchwarden were esteemed roles that were filled by contested elections, with several candidates standing. Today, the role is now so burdensome and demanding, and lacks esteem, that few, if any, will volunteer for this. A significant number of Church of England parishes are now unable to meet the legal requirement for two churchwardens. Some parishes cannot find anyone to do the role.

There is some cognitive dissonance at work here. A bishop turning up at a church that has not been able to obtain ordained ministry for some time and is looking at an extended season without a clergyperson, may well believe that stressing 'every-member ministry' will land as good news for the congregation, and even feel quite liberating. However, I suspect that telling a congregation that they can minister to one another, and practise this upon the wider community, is more akin to telling an adult education class that they will benefit from being without a qualified lecturer offering expertise and specific educational input, and the class can teach themselves just as well and recruit others to such classes too.

If the bishop then adds that the course fees are still going to rise, even though this adult education class is now also responsible for their own teaching, curriculum, validation and paying for the maintenance of the buildings, lay ministry does not look quite so attractive. That feeling of being 'set free' and empowerment that the bishop said they would experience – the proverbial miracle of 'less is more' – will surely only present as some cruel chimera.

Put bluntly, the work of God – opus Dei – is hard and laborious, and not many want to get involved. It's always been like this. Jesus said as much (c.f. Matthew 9.35–38). Offering TLC – tender, loving care – is not a carrot on the end of a recruitment stick. The other TLC – time, labour, cash – is what churches struggle to deal with in the midst of secularization and religious recession. Trying to spiritually blackmail the laity into plugging all the gaps is unlikely to work. The laity, in any case, are pretty busy being at work in the world, and are not some free labour supply that the church can call upon to supplement the needs of the church at the beck and call of the bishop. I recall a recent stand-off between an archdeacon who refused to work evenings and insisted on meeting the churchwardens during a weekday in office hours. The wardens explained that they had jobs. They offered Saturday (reluctantly, as it was their family time). The archdeacon replied that Saturday was a day off too, so not willing to diarize anything that day. Eighteen months later, no date had been fixed.

Harold Wilson (1916–95), the Labour Party Prime Minister in the 1960s, when asked, 'How many people have you got working for you here?' is alleged to have quipped, 'About half.' The truth is that not every follower of Jesus or member of a church regards themselves as an underutilized disciple or even as a lay minister-in-waiting.

Re-reading the Gospels

Secularization has led to the profound depletion of belief and belonging among faith communities. Churches, therefore, struggle with decline. But to state the obvious, it does not follow that the answer to decline is growth. As will be apparent in these lesson notes, I take issue with the prevailing credo and dogma that asserts the church's primary calling is to grow, and the primary calling of Christians is to 'make (more) disciples', and that this is how secularization and contemporary experiences of religious recession are best addressed.

What is so beguiling about growth-related social, missional and spiritual constructions of reality is that this seems obvious and indisputable in the face of declining congregations in the northern hemisphere (across all traditions and even among evangelicals and charismatics, with more indications of stalling than success). But we should be particularly alert at precisely such moments, for the most obvious solutions to theological and ecclesial conundrums can often flirt with or be subsumed into subtle half-heresies.

Ecclesiology is only our Christology that is worked out in practice. The mission is encountering the Spirit within and beyond the church. Who we think Jesus is and how we encounter and experience his transformation of us is what leads to the formation of the church. Likewise, how a congregation senses, understands, reflects upon and reifies the power of the Holy Spirit and the presence of God is what church is. Priorities, prayer, worship, study, hospitality, community building, receptivity, kindness, care, love, joy and peacebuilding will all flow from this. No church can ever be more than a fallen, fragile and flawed manifestation of Christ.

There is a small but growing resistance to the mechanistic-productive models of the church, which have dominated popular approaches to ecclesiology, mission and ministry in the post-war era. Daniel Guder's missiological and ecclesial assessment articulates what many critics of the church-growth movement are thinking. Namely, that for all the apparent success, there is an underlying functionalism that may be doing significant damage to the organic nature of ecclesial polity. The apparent success may, in fact, turn out to be a significant betrayal of identity and undermine the actual mission of the church:

> The more the Church is treated as an organization, the more its mission becomes focused on techniques designed to maximize output and productivity. We become obsessed with quantity instead of quality, and where we have a care for quality, it is only to serve the larger goal of increasing quantity. The Church moves to becoming a managed machine, with its managers judging their performance by growth-related metrics. (Guder, *Called to Witness*, p. 37)

The call to return to models of local, organic, authentic and small-scale parishes that are rooted and grounded in their contexts is still only a movement with a faint pulse. However, I sense that the mechanistic-productive model is ageing, failing and losing its agency – though cultural-missional hubris, a lack of theological wisdom and deteriorating spiritual self-awareness mask this from its proponents.

The Church as a Manufacturer of Disciples

For an illustration of this, the Archbishop of York's address on 30 July at the 2022 Lambeth Conference is even more revealing:

> McDonalds make hamburgers. Starbucks make coffee ... Heineken make beer. Toyota make cars. Rolex make watches ... and, sisters and brothers, the Church of Jesus Christ makes disciples. That is our core business. That is what we are about. Not just converts. Jesus doesn't say 'go into the world and make converts'. He doesn't say 'go into the world and make churchgoers'. He says 'make disciples'. Followers of Jesus.

The archepiscopal stress is placed on productivity, but with the bishops (to paraphrase Marx) controlling the means of production. True, Marx said it was the 'workers' who controlled the means of production, and I daresay the Archbishop hopes it will be the laity – his workers – who will deliver on the targets he sets, with all increased productivity lightly supervised and energized by compliant clergy. Here, the robotic, simplistic and mechanistic analogy for the church imagines a seamless linearity between raw material, goods produced and consumer take-up. Of course, this is not exactly what Marx had in mind in *The Communist Manifesto*, where the workers, post-revolution, were to be accorded equality in deciding on production priorities and outputs, and otherwise have full agency in their economic, political and social self-determination.

True, we might well hope that disciples could be an objective, or even a consequence, of the mission of the church. However, disciples are not the 'product' or the 'output' of what the churches are offering. That would be tantamount to claiming that the purpose and product of a business was satisfied customers. That is plainly wrong. The product is the goods or services that the business provides, based on its purposes, which only then might lead to customers 'being satisfied'.

But there are other reasons to query the consumerist-production model of discipleship. Leaving aside the fact that 'discipleship' does not occur as a term in the New Testament, we have to face up to the morally ambivalent histories of these mega-corporations (e.g. lack of union rights for workers and low pay; participation in making military hardware for the Axis powers in the Second World War; alcohol, addiction and sports sponsorship, with links to gambling). On reading the commission of Matthew 28, a twenty-first-century, culturally relative consumer might assume that 'make disciples' means 'make' in the sense of manufacture, production or multiplicity. A momentary expository pause would suggest that even when just taking an English translation, other things one can 'make' include apologies, peace, excuses, or even 'make good'. Surely the task of the church is not to 'make' anything but, first and foremost, to 'bear witness'.

The witness of such a church might lead to depletion, colossal persecution and martyrdom. Or a sustained period of being unfashionable, not the flavour of the month, year, or even decade. That sort of season would put most companies out of business. And the church is not a business. But if productivity is now being made 'core' to the identity and integrity of the church, it will collapse into becoming little more than a business. (Incidentally, very few companies last a hundred years, let alone two thousand.)

The Greek phrase for 'make disciples' only occurs in three other places in the New Testament (*mathēteuō*, which comes from *mathētēs*, meaning 'disciple'). In all cases, the Greek alludes to an established teacher–learner relationship, more usually associated with lengthy periods of apprenticeship and education. Furthermore, and this should perhaps be obvious, very few followers of Jesus were disciples. But all disciples were followers. The text, therefore, is not about conversion of the masses. Rather, it is about educating the few (i.e. the disciples) to reach outside the realms of Galilee and Jerusalem ('the nations').

Likewise, 'go and make disciples …' would be better rendered as 'in your going' or 'as you return/depart back to Jerusalem, remember to …'. This commission from Jesus links to the earlier one in the upper room, and the call to the disciples here is to shift their mission from being ethnocentric to becoming *ektocentric* – outfacing and global, and now a faith that is no longer concerned with remaining within Judaism. True, the disciples will return to 'the Temple' to praise God. However, thereafter, their task is to reach beyond the Temple, just as Jesus witnessed to the Gentiles. They must embrace their exile.

Any notion that this passage can sustain and support an exegesis that christens 'mass-production', extensive evangelism and conversion as the primary intent is absurd. Let alone this being *the* 'Great Commission' Jesus signs off with. It is not original to the biblical text. The 'Great

Commission' is clearly an added subtitle that crept into many translations of scripture during the era of intense missionary and colonial endeavour in the early nineteenth century. This subtitle was not featured in earlier translations of scripture, and it did not debut as a phrase with earlier generations of missionaries.

In fact, Matthew 28 does not mention conversion, though careful readers of the passage will note that there is an order to outline for disciples as they go about their way. First, baptize them. Second, teach them to observe those things that are needed in following Jesus.

Every disciple is a Christian, but not every Christian is a disciple. Just as every apostle was a follower, but not every follower was an apostle. Everyone who drives a car or needs to tell the time does not need to own a Rolex or drive a Toyota – or even own a car or have a watch.

The mechanistic-productive model is a temptation, to be sure – a kind of heretical imperative. Especially in times of sparsity, when the church only seems to experience increasing decline and disinterest. However, there is less scriptural warrant for Church-Growth-Centric ecclesial paradigms than many suppose, and Matthew 28 is not a conversionist or production-orientated text.

Resisting Capitalist Culture in the Church

Christianity is a duty and a joy as practised. Yet few who practise it will ever see easy and obvious productive outcomes. The church may have many followers, but only a very few are called to be a disciple. The Gospels bear this out too. Jesus had many followers, and cared for them as much as his most devoted disciples – the latter being very few in number. The early church was no different. The history of the church bears this out. A few have vocations. The many just want to follow. God loves them all, equally.

Thus, there needs to be a reset in the minds of church leaders as to who and what can be counted on. The church is tasked with learning the Christological grammar that rules faithful speech and thought about the person and nature of Jesus Christ.

This might seem sufficient as a critique, in effect, framing church-growth thinking within the ecology of capitalism. But Bishop Lesslie Newbigin turned the critique into something altogether more surprising in *Foolishness to the Greeks*:

> Modern capitalism has created a world totally different from anything known before. Previous ages have assumed that resources are limited and that economics – housekeeping – is about how to distribute them fairly. Since Adam Smith, we have learned to assume that exponential growth is the basic law of economics and that no limits can be set to it. (p. 38)

The result is that increased production has become an end in itself. If the church becomes stuck in a mode of productivity, it will quickly find that those same products are destined to become rapidly obsolete. The metaphor of the church as a body is therefore quite deliberate in the New Testament; it is not a machine designed to produce results (Romans 12.5; I Corinthians 12.12–27; Ephesians 3.6 and 5.23; Colossians 1.18 and 1.24). So Newbigin continues:

> Growth is for the sake of growth and is not determined by any overarching social purpose. And that, of course, is an exact account of the phenomenon which, when it occurs in the human body, is called cancer. In the long perspective of history, it would be difficult to deny that the exuberant capitalism of the past 250 years will be diagnosed in the future as a desperately dangerous case of cancer in the body of human society – if indeed this cancer has not been terminal and there are actually survivors around to make the diagnosis. (p. 38)

For Christians, living is bound up in the life, death and resurrection of Jesus. Therefore, our lives are to be, in a real sense, lived sacrificially and vicariously. In John 12.24ff., we are reminded that the 'grain of wheat must fall' for new and greater growth. As is so often the case with the scriptures, translations and the passage of time do not always serve us well. The Greek word John gives us is not 'dies', but rather 'decays' or 'rots'.

Moreover, the seed does not actually 'die'. It is dormant once separated from the stalk ('falls to the ground'), and it is only when the kernel begins to decay that the seed can germinate. Put another way, Jesus does not speak of a lifeless death in John 12.24ff. Instead, he invites us to ponder what must decay and rot to enhance some more abundant life. That means letting go of linear, agribusiness mechanistic-productive models of church growth, and re-engaging with the seasonal cycles of organic life (and death) that yield faithful fecundity.

John 12.25 concludes by telling us, 'Those who love their life lose it, and those who hate their life in this world will keep it for eternal life.'

FUTURE DIRECTIONS: WHAT3WORDS? GO, MAKE, DISCIPLES

The Greek word for 'life' is *zōē*, but the word used in this saying of Jesus is *psychē* (or soul). 'Hate' (*miseō*) seems like a relatively strong word to use against the seat of your own consciousness. Still, scholars agree that the word in Jesus' saying is about distancing yourself from self-admiration, self-regard and self-preservation.

Love (*agapē*), as we know, is the converging force that draws elements and people together towards unity. *Miseō*, in contrast, is a divergent force that enlarges the spaces, gaps and divisions between us. *Miseō* diminishes togetherness, shared knowledge and 'knowing' (spiritual, sexual or social).

Put another way, the more we indulge our needs at the expense of others, the greater the distances between us will be. The church is not called to self-love, even motivated by self-pity or self-preservation. Only love for God and love for others will close the gaps that have opened within our churches, and the chasms that now exist between the church and the world.

Summary

The primary problem with Christians 'making' disciples is that the embedded notions of manufacture, commodification and replacing unity with machined uniformity are hard to escape. They are 'baked in' to the formulaic conceptuality. Interestingly, a growing number of teachers in homiletics, ministry studies and pastoral theology have been helped by Wendell Berry's work and writings on land, agriculture and attention to the local.

As proponents of minor, authentic, organic-local churches have consistently argued, when the local church lives out this vocation faithfully, the congregations and parishes are encountered as genuine, authentic and transformative. They are faithful expressions of their local community and the Spirit of Christ. In their incarnation, they become incorporative.

So, the gospel is the seed. We may be the kernel. Yet if so, we have no real use other than to become detached from the sap-giving stem and to fall. Yet we cling on for dear life, even though we know that we need to learn to fall, be cracked open, and slowly decay so that the seed can germinate. We are not the seed. We are not the gospel.

My what3words app offers no 1m-square location on the planet corresponding to 'go.make.disciples'. That address is unknown – not a point of departure, let alone for any destination. In the meantime, the calling for all Christians is to love, surrender, serve and be dug into the ground where God has placed us. It is what Jesus did. It is a profoundly embodied and organic vision.

Prospects: Onwards and Upwards?

One reason for pursuing a confessional and an academic agenda in this book (i.e. combining sociology, ecclesiology, faith and contemporary culture) is that the enterprise itself is largely counter-cultural within the churches. Since the early 1960s, both the academy and the widespread public imagination have been in the grip of secularization theories, namely the simple assertion that as society progressively becomes more modern, so will it lose its religious heritage and interests. However, a significant amount of revisionism occurred in the last half of the twentieth century and the first quarter of the twenty-first century.

Most scholars have realized that modernization can often heighten the role of religion on the public stage. That said, no one can survey contemporary cultural life, at least in Western Europe, and conclude that religion is as strong as it once was. But neither is it evaporating in the way that sociologists of religion once predicted. In truth, the socio-cultural changes are more complex than any single or simple secularization theory can normally enunciate. But what, then, are the factors that have prompted cultural and religious change, as churches and faiths move forward? Several brief points need making here.

First, the rise of religious pluralism has had a marked impact on religion over the past three centuries. However, this pluralism plays out differently across the continents. In Britain, the passing of the 1689 Toleration Act seriously undermined the grounds for enforcing uniform religious practice on the population. 'Dissenting traditions' steadily gained in number and influence, and this weakened the grip of 'state' religion.

Second, the impact of religious pluralism in America had a quite different effect. The absence of officially sanctioned religion for the populace led to a flourishing culture of religious competition that still thrives today. Religion is part of the overall commodification of

American life, and choices, as in so many spheres of ordinary life, closely identify individuals and communities. Around 25% of the population go to church and many more identify with a denomination or place of worship. However, as we have seen, this is depleting.

Third, Western Europe witnessed a gradual but persistent loosening of ties between church and state. This led to the gradual decrease in the power of the churches in prominent spheres of public life. In turn, this led to a decline in religious practice, which was only occasionally halted by popular revivals and other movements. (However, Europe is the exception, globally, not the rule. For the rest of the world, religious revival and growth is comparatively normal, even with the growth of modernization and consumerism.)

Fourth, there has been a general agenda of social 'liberalizing' throughout the past century. Laws on abortion, obscenity, marriage, divorce and homosexuality have all correlated with a set of cultural, political and social trends that have seen religion pushed from the place of control within the public sphere to one that is more private. Increasingly, performing religious tasks, duties and rituals is seen as something 'private' undertaken in leisure time. Fewer and fewer Roman Catholics attend confession regularly; holy days of obligation, unless they fall on Sundays, are unlikely to be keenly observed.

Fifth, the decline of associations in general has had a deleterious impact upon religious institutions. Although scholars such as Grace Davie have suggested that religion has fared better than, say, trade unions, it remains the case that modern Western society (including America) is entering a 'post-associational' state. Individuals in society are increasingly disconnected from one another, as 'soft' social structures such as the Masons, Odd Fellows, Women's Institutes have rapidly disintegrated. What has replaced these social ties is consumerism and the 'negative social capital' of television and other forms of media, which have become the new electronic public sphere.

Sixth, there is an increasing fluidity about how religious, moral and political beliefs are held within modernity. Consumerism infects not only practice and adherence, but also alters the landscape of belief. Few Christians in the West, even those committed to various forms of conservative belief, will subscribe to literal interpretations of biblical stories or historic understandings of doctrines such as hell. In what Bauman calls our 'liquid modernity', more fluid forms of association and belief have sprung up, which, while still allowing for the possibility of metanarratives, nonetheless relate to them differently in the twenty-first century.

Seventh, and finally, the rise of spiritualities – in their superfluous 'alternative', 'vernacular', 'folk' and other forms – continues questioning secularization theories' dominance on the academy landscape and the public imagination. France, where secularity is profound and pervasive, can still boast 40,000 fortune-tellers. Most British newspapers (not just the tabloids) will have a daily or weekly horoscope fronted by a renowned astrologer. Spirituality is a more fluid (modern?) and pervasive expression of the religious sentiments that continue to shape everyday life in myriad ways. Theological engagements with culture, then, need to take a severe account of the grounded reality of religion in its typical contexts and situations and not simply engage with religion conceptually or as a 'high' and overly defined culture.

But where does this leave the church? There is no dispute that churchgoing has declined in most Western countries since the 1960s. Although it is currently the fashion to talk about European exceptionalism here, the USA was unusual since declines in churchgoing can be tracked in Australia, New Zealand and many other places. But as we know, and as sociologists remind us, the statistics we have cannot be read 'simply'; the complex data demands an equally complex interpretation, and if we are to hold our nerve as a church within contemporary culture, we must have robust cultural understandings of our current situation. Robin Gill suggests that there are four possible theories that have implications for churchgoing (see Gill, *Theology in a Social Context*; *Theology Shaped by Society*; *Society Shaped by Theology*).

First, *secularization* theories – especially those espoused by Steve Bruce, Callum Brown, the early work of Peter Berger and the offerings of the late Bryan Wilson. However, many sociologists have demonstrated, both from a theoretical and empirical perspective, that crude or blunt secularization theories are inadequate in their interpretation of churchgoing habits.

Second, *persistence* theories exist, as offered by Rodney Stark, David Martin and myself. Here, the argument runs that although there is detachment from religion's duties and formal obligations, it nonetheless persists as part of public life. Correspondingly, scholars such as José Casanova show that religion can decline and persist simultaneously; where religion loses influence in the intensive and specific spheres of public life, it often makes up for the loss in extensive attraction, and this movement can flow the other way, too.

Third, and perhaps developing theories one and two, there are *separation* theories – perhaps best represented by Grace Davie, Peter Berger's more recent work, and with Anthony Giddens and Reginald Bibby also contributing. Here, the critical point to acknowledge is the gap that has opened up between believing and belonging, the latter having declined while the former mutates and, at the very least, holds its own.

Fourth, and finally, Gill suggests that a *cultural* theory needs to be explored. Here, Gill indicates that churches, as moral communities, do hold and foster distinctive beliefs and values that, in turn, sustain individual and community identity. Correspondingly, a decline in belonging will inevitably lead to a decline in beliefs. If belonging collapses, the community and authority that sustains the beliefs cannot continue in the same way. The churches are discovering this, not least with the alarming rate of decline in religious literacy.

That said, secularization theories need to be handled with great care. As we have seen, even if we think we are experiencing secularization and that our faith, beliefs and churches are caught in the grip of it, all is not as it seems on the surface. And all is not lost. It is certainly the case that the 1960s was a defining decade for the churches, and I wonder if many have yet to come to terms with the social dynamics the era ushered in, let alone recover and learn from it. Hugh McLeod's *The Religious Crisis of the 1960s* offers something of an antidote to the likes of Steve Bruce and Callum Brown, and here I think McLeod can help us reframe our understanding of secularization. I list ten brief points here to sum up our findings on secularization.

1 The term is loaded, and can often be a 'tool of counter-religious ideologies'; a way of framing history that is 'spun'.
2 Adoption of the term often leads to the thesis directing the facts – actually, what is the evidence for long-term religious decline?
3 Secularization often means little more than 'religious change' – for example on gender, divorce or sexuality.
4 There is also a question of how to interpret the growth of alternative spirituality and new patterns of belonging/believing.
5 The movement from Christendom (or Christian country) to 'civilized society' is not necessarily irreversible, or even less and/or anti-religious.
6 Church attendance figures do not tell the whole story – of intensive versus extensive religion, and of market versus utility, for example.
7 Religion may have become more of a 'product' or 'resource' in modernity – something to improve life, etc.; but is this 'secularization'?
8 Religions are not immune from contextual development, generational shifts, etc. – the key one in Europe is change in patterns of belonging.

9 The 1960s may turn out to be a decade for shaping and defining modern religion, but all Christians have always lived in modern times.
10 There are many causes for the decline and rise of religion – each age is pregnant with the next, and by many sources, spores and seeds (David Martin, *The Breaking of the Image*, p. 2).

Secularization has become a contemporary Christian obsession, and as a credo is endorsed as though an article of faith. Like many obsessions, the outward appearance is more attractive than the contents. Many Christians appear to believe that secularization is some external hindrance that accounts for their waning support. In truth, church leaders are largely responsible for how Christian faith looks to the world, and secularization is hardly an external force or rival to the church that has some impact on the integrity of belief. The church has become consumed with how it appears to the world. Self-absorbed, it has secularized itself without needing much in the way of external support.

But Christians are committed to the doctrine of the incarnation. Jesus was born into a world of powers, authorities, customs, practices, cultures and histories from which he was not separated. In becoming human and one of us, he then finds faith in the 'secular' world around him, outside Jewish territories, and in people and places that know nothing of Judaism, let alone Christianity. As such, Jesus, in his life, work and ministry, not only bridges the perceived tribal and ideological boundaries of the secular and sacred realms but sets about dissolving them at every opportunity. The Holy Spirit continues that work. Christians now find God in the secular. The secular is not some rival agency that threatens to overrun religion. On the contrary, the secular is now precisely the place where Christians are expected to encounter the work of the Holy Spirit.

This may all sound too much for some Christians because the church has groomed believers into thinking that they possess the truth and that the world knows nothing of God. Again, we must reckon with what the first Christians understood by faith. We moderns think of it as belief, meaning a set of dry doctrinal and rational propositions. But the Greek word for 'faith' (*pistis*) in the New Testament is better rendered as 'trust in' or 'divine persuasion', rather than 'believe' or 'belief'. Thus, John 3.16 is better read as 'for God so loved the world that he gave his one and only Son, that whoever trusts in him shall not perish but have eternal life'.

Faith and trust sit within the economy of fear and anxiety that was so prevalent in the ancient world. We see this expressed in the two different words used by Jesus to indicate fear. In Mark 4.35–41, Jesus calms the storm and mildly chides the disciples with a rhetorical question: 'Why are you so afraid? Have you still no faith?' (verse 40, ESV). The disciples' reaction to the calming of the storm, is however, that they 'were filled with great fear and said to one another, 'Who then is this, that even the wind and the sea obey him?' (verse 41, ESV).

To us moderns, fear is just fear. But the two words used in the Gospel text are subtly different. In verse 40, Jesus asks why the disciples are so *deilos*, which is better translated as 'timid'. In verse 41, the disciples are fearful, with the Greek word this time being *phobeō*, from which we derive phobia – irrational terror and fears, such as of spiders or space (arachnophobia or agoraphobia).

The question, I guess, is why Jesus asks about the timidity of the disciples when their boat seems about to sink? They are unlikely to be good swimmers, so not unreasonably may fear drowning. But *deilos* is not fear – it is anxiety, apprehensiveness, concern, worrying and fretting. Timidity is a kind of paralysis – the courage sucked dry before the threat is even engaged with. Time and time again, Jesus exhorts his disciples not to have *deilos*, as it produces nothing but paralysing fear (phobia). We are not to worry about what to wear, what to eat, or the unknowns of tomorrow. If we do, today will never happen.

Christians are meant to live by trust in the present moment. Although Jesus never said this (to the best of our knowledge), the lesson on fear and trust in the Gospels can be summed up as 'Keep calm and carry on'. The church may have to adopt that as a mission slogan in the face of the storms of secularization. Calmness is what Christ brings. Continuity is our response. It doesn't mean Christians 'carry on' as though nothing need change, or everything must be repeated. On the contrary, 'carry on' means commitment to living in a future that does not leave us paralysed by the present. Christianity is not 'at ease, as you were'. It is, rather, 'attention, as you should be'. Stay alert.

It is not possible to accurately predict how religion will shape society or be shaped by it. Religion is an adaptive, regulative framework, and as Charles Taylor notes carefully some denominations are *consequences* of class division and increased social mobilization. Furthermore, the increased mobility brought about through modernity and industrialization makes possible new communities of affinity that are no longer contingent on locality. Religious movements come and go; intensity usually slides into eventual extensity (e.g. bureaucratization and routinization in charismatic renewal movements), but this is not about secular forces dissipating faith.

Like life itself, religion goes through cycles and constantly changes and renews itself. Religion has always been living in the secular. As we noted at the start of this book, the Latin and Greek roots of 'secular' are concerned with temporality, ages, eras, generations and lifespan. The secular is not eternal. Like religion, it ties things together to make meaning and values and points beyond itself to an age yet to come. So, the period of late modernity we generally regard as the 'secular age' might merely be a blip on our social landscape. This is just one phase in the long, complex history of humanity, churches, religions, faiths and their evolutions within societies. We have no idea if we are near the end of this – or barely begun.

So, onwards it is. The pilgrim church will keep going. Its fate seems destined to be more minor, less well regarded and more marginal. Any upward trend seems unlikely. The best hope for the trajectory ahead will be some levelling out of the decline faith communities are experiencing. I fear we are nowhere near that yet and have further to descend. However, for all the steep fall-offs noted, we must remember that they do not necessarily lead to some final, fatal terminal for spirituality and faith within contemporary culture and society.

Religion, like life, is full of surprises. Rumours of Jesus' resurrection will continue to haunt today's secular powers as in the days of Pilate. The resurrection confounds those who scribbled 'The End' and wrote off the possibility of any sequel. The hubris of secularization is failing to realize and understand that this one death merely marked the beginning of something entirely new. A future that would burst all frames of reference and perplex those who had predicted the demise of God. Certainly, churches and the Christian faith face enormous challenges going forward in the twenty-first century. But is now really the time to be writing 'RIP Religion'? Honestly, I do not think so.

From the Librarian: References and Further Reading

References

Raymond Aron, *Main Currents in Sociological Thought*, Penguin, 1970.
Edward Bailey, *Implicit Religion in Contemporary Society*, Kok Pharos, 1997.
Jenna Bailey, *Can Any Mother Help Me?*, Faber & Faber, 2007.
J. G. Ballard, *The Drowned World*, Doubleday, 1965.
Peter Berger, *Invitation to Sociology*, Doubleday, 1963.
Peter Berger, *The Desecularization of the World*, Eerdmans, 1999.
Peter Berger and Thomas Luckmann, *The Social Construction of Reality*, Penguin, 1967.
Lieven Boeve, *Interrupting Tradition: An Essay on Christian Faith in a Postmodern Context*, Louvain Theological and Pastoral Monographs, 30, Peeters, 2003.
Raymond Boyle, 'Football and Religion: Merseyside and Glasgow', in Stephen Hopkins, Cathy Long and John Williams, eds, *Passing Rhythms: Liverpool FC and the Transformation of Football*, Bloomsbury, 2001.
Steve Bruce, *Religion and Modernisation*, Oxford University Press, 1992.
Sylvia Collins, 'Spirituality and Youth', in Martyn Percy, ed., *Calling Time: Religion and Change at the Turn of the Millennium*, Sheffield Academic Press, 2000.
James Corbett, 'Bill Shankly: Life, death and football', *The Observer*, 18 October 2009.
Grace Davie, 'Believing without Belonging: A Liverpool Case Study', *Archives de Sciences Sociales des Religions* (38e Année, No. 81, January–March 1993, pp. 79–89.
Grace Davie, *Religion in Britain Since 1945: Believing Without Belonging*, Blackwell, 1994.
Jim Davies, Michael Graham and Ryan Burge, *The Great Dechurching*, Zondervan, 2023.

Kenda Creasy Dean, *Almost Christian: What the Faith of Our Teenagers is Telling the Church*, Oxford University Press, 2010.

Paulo Freire, *Pedagogy of the Oppressed*, trans. Myra Bergman Ramos, Herder and Herder, 1970.

Anthony Giddens, *The Consequences of Modernity*, Polity Press, 1991.

Robin Gill, *Theology in a Social Context*, Ashgate, 2012; *Theology Shaped by Society*, Ashgate, 2012; *Society Shaped by Theology*, Ashgate, 2013.

Darrell Guder, *Called to Witness: Doing Missional Theology*, Eerdmans, 2015.

Mathew Guest, Kristin Aune, Sonya Sharma and Rob Warner, *Christianity and the University Experience: Understanding Student Faith*, Bloomsbury Academic, 2013.

Os Guinness, *The Last Christian on Earth: Uncover the Enemy's Plot to Undermine the Church*, Baker Books, 2010; 1st edn published as Os Guinness, *The Gravedigger File*, Hodder & Stoughton, 1983.

Tomáš Halík, *The Afternoon of Christianity*, Notre Dame University Press, 2024.

Nick Hornby, *Fever Pitch*, Gollancz, 1992.

Robert P. Jones, *White Too Long: The Legacy of White Supremacy in American Christianity*, Simon & Schuster, 2020.

Robert P. Jones, *The End of White Christian America*, Simon & Schuster, 2016.

Robin Kent, *Aunt Agony Advises: Problem Pages Through the Ages*, W. H. Allen, 1979.

Ursula Le Guin, *Dancing at the Edge of the World: Thoughts on Words, Women, Places*, Grove Books, 1989.

David Lodge, *How Far Can You Go?*, Secker & Warburg, 1980.

David Martin, *The Breaking of the Image: A Sociology of Christian Theory and Practice*, Blackwell, 1980.

David Martin, 'Believing without Belonging', cited in Grace Davie, *Religion in Britain Since 1945*, Blackwell, 1994.

Peter Mayo, *Gramsci, Freire, and Adult Education: Possibilities for Transformative Action*, Zed Books, 1999.

Eugene McCarraher, *The Enchantments of Mammon: How Capitalism Became the Religion of Modernity*, Belknap Press, 2019.

Hugh McLeod, *The Religious Crisis of the 1960s*, Oxford University Press, 2007.

John Milbank, *The Word Made Strange: Theology, Language, Culture*, Blackwell, 1997.

Graham Neville, *Radical Churchman: Edward Lee Hicks and the New Liberalism*, Clarendon, 1998.
Lesslie Newbigin, *Foolishness to the Greeks*, SPCK, 1986.
H. Richard Niebuhr, *Christ and Culture*, Harper, 1951.
Robert Nisbet, *The Sociological Tradition*, Basic Books, 1966.
Michael Novak, *The Joy of Sports: End Zones, Bases, Baskets, Balls, and the Consecration of the American Spirit*, Hamilton, 1976, rev. edn, Madison, 1993.
Martyn Percy, 'Consecrated Pragmatism', *Anvil*, Vol. 14, No. 1, 1997.
Martyn Percy, *The Humble Church: Becoming the Body of Christ*, Canterbury Press, 2021.
Martyn Percy, *The Precarious Church: Redeeming the Body of Christ*, Canterbury Press, 2023.
Mike Pilavachi, *Soul Survivor*, Regal Books, 2004.
Joseph Pine and James Gilmore, 'Welcome to the Experience Economy', *Harvard Business Review*, July–August, 1998, pp. 12–25.
Michael Sadgrove, 'Evensong', *The Prayer Book Today*, The Magazine of the Prayer Society, Issue 4, Lent 2017, pp. 11–12.
Peter Schmiechen, *Christ the Reconciler: A Theology for Opposites, Differences and Enemies*, Eerdmans, 1996.
Peter Schmiechen, *Saving Power: Theories of Atonement and Forms of the Church*, Eerdmans, 2005.
Larry Shiner, 'The Concept of Secularization in Empirical Research', *Journal for the Scientific Study of Religion*, Vol. 6, No. 2, 1967, pp. 207–20.
Charles. J. Somerville, *The Secularization of Early Modern England: From Religious Culture to Religious Faith*, Oxford University Press, 1992.
Luzia Sutter Rehmann, *Rage in the Belly: Hunger in the New Testament*, trans. Monica Buckland, Cascade, 2021.
Charles Taylor, *A Secular Age*, Belknap Press/Harvard University Press, 2007.
Rick Warren, *The Purpose Driven Life: What on Earth Am I Here For?*, Zondervan, 2002.
John Wimber, *Signs and Wonders and Church Growth*, Harper & Row, 1988.
Charles Wright Mills, *The Sociological Imagination*, Oxford University Press, 1959.

Introductions

Before engaging with texts on secularization, it pays well to read some of the historical and cultural studies that address the mixed fortunes of the churches in the twentieth and twenty-first centuries. One of the most esteemed and enduring studies in the field is *Churches and Churchgoers*, written by the esteemed trio of Robert Currie, Alan Gilbert and Lee Horsley (Oxford University Press, 1977). This seminal work meticulously traces the ebb and flow of British churchgoing from the Victorian era to 1970, standing as a beacon of scholarly excellence.

In recent years, Clive Field has emerged as a scholarly powerhouse, producing works that are not only exceptional but also timely. His work, *Counting Religion in Britain 1970–2020: Secularization in Statistical Context* (Oxford University Press, 2021), serves as the definitive guide to the religious trends of the past half-century. His earlier works, *Periodizing Secularization: Religious Allegiance and Attendance in Britain, 1880–1945* (Oxford University Press, 2019) and *Secularization in the Long 1960s: Numerating Religion in Britain* (Oxford University Press, 2017), are equally noteworthy. All works by Hugh McLeod, such as *The Religious Crisis of the 1960s* (Oxford University Press, 2007), are also highly recommended.

Over the past few centuries, establishment institutions have faced a crisis, a phenomenon that Kenneth Thompson astutely observed in his *Bureaucracy and Church Reform: The Organizational Response of the Church of England to Social Change, 1800 to 1965* (Oxford University Press, 1970). The Church of England has experienced a social shrinkage, transforming into a more peripheral and less extensive institution. For those interested in understanding how class, ethnicity and other factors influence state churches' evolution, devolution and decline, H. R. Niebuhr's *The Social Sources of Denominationalism* (Henry Holt & Co., 1929) is an excellent starting point. It is also worth looking at Conrad Ostwalt's *Secular Steeples: Popular Culture and the Religious Imagination* (Trinity Press International, 2003).

Martyn Percy's *Clergy: The Origin of Species* (T&T Clark, 2006) and *The Crisis of Colonial Anglicanism: Slavery, Revolt, Empire and the Church of England* (Hurst, 2026) provide further insights. Mady Thung's *The Precarious Organisation* (Mouton & Co., 1976) remains one of the most comprehensive accounts of the reasons for church decline in the modern era, a must-read alongside Loren Mead's *The Once and the Future Church* (Alban, 1991) and Gibson Winter's *The Suburban Captivity of the Churches* (Macmillan, 1962).

On geography in general, we commend the work of Tim Marshall, and in particular *The Future of Geography* (Elliott & Thompson Ltd., 2023). As space frontiers open and telecommunications are no longer dependent on national borders, this is as good an introduction as any to how faith groups might adapt to secularization. Over the last 50 years, religious TV channels have been beamed from space and have had a niche influence.

David Hackett Fischer's *Albion's Seed: Four British Folkways in America* (Oxford University Press, 1989) provides a careful historical study of the development of early Christianity in America. Although Robin Niblett's *The New Cold War* (Atlantic Books, 2024) does not explicitly comment on religion, the emerging contest between China and the USA will involve some faith-related challenges shaping the twenty-first century.

Hugh Turpin, an anthropologist at Oxford and a scholar at the Centre for the Study of Social Cohesion, explains the demographics of growing secularization in Ireland across the counties. His *Unholy Catholic Ireland: Religious Hypocrisy, Secular Morality and Irish Irreligion* (Stanford University Press, 2022) is an excellent study in secularization 'flipping' Catholic Christianity when it is perceived to have inflicted extensive moral injury on its people.

Ekaterina Kolpinskaya and Stuart Fox account for the geographic factors in recent British political turbulence, with their *Religion and Euroscepticism in Brexit Britain* (Routledge, 2021). More parochially, there are numerous studies of the Church of England engaged in self-secularizing through anxious reforms that only lead to greater disenchantment and disinvestment. Alison Milbank's *The Once and Future Parish* (SCM Press, 2023) is among the best of them.

Three good texts on Scottish religion are Callum Brown's *Religion and Society in Scotland Since 1707* (Edinburgh University Press, 1997 and 2007), Steve Bruce's *Scottish Gods: Religion in Modern Scotland, 1900–2012* (Edinburgh University Press, 2014 and 2016), and Doug Gay's *Reforming the Kirk: The Future of the Church of Scotland* (Saint Andrew Press, 2017), based on his delivery of the Chalmers Lectures. For social, historical and geographical background, *Scotland: The Autobiography*, ed. Rosemary Goering (Penguin, 2008) and *Who Are The Scots?*, ed. Gordon Menzies (Edinburgh University Press, 2002) are among the best.

Four seminal texts from David Martin's distinguished corpus that I have cherished over the years that are historically nuanced include *The Sociology of English Religion* (SCM Press, 1967); *The Breaking of the Image* (Blackwell, 1980); *Christian Language and its Mutations* (Ashgate, 2002); and *Christian Language and the Secular City* (Ashgate, 2002). Within the field of the sociology of religion, David Martin was a colossus. Martin's critiques of secularization – for which he is probably best known – began early in his academic career. His first significant study ('Notes for a General Theory of Secularisation', 1969) was later published as *A General Theory of Secularisation* (Oxford University Press, 1978). This remains one of the landmark texts in the history of secularization studies. Few scholars in the post-war era had intellectual sensitivity towards English religion.

Even in retirement, Martin contributed to debates on secularization and religion's surprising resilience in the twenty-first century. Martin argued that there was some evidence of resilience, mutations and effervescence in modern religion with the growth of Pentecostalism. His work has looked at Latin America's developing economies and new urban sprawls to show how religion can grow and prosper in modern societies.

Rodney Stark's *The Triumph of Christianity: How the Jesus Movement Became the World's Largest Religion* (Harper, 2011) and his *The Triumph of Faith: Why the World Is More Religious than Ever* (Harper, 2015) will assist the reader in gaining a more extended and broader historical context for current debates on secularization in the developed world.

Secularization and spiritual salience in contemporary culture

Larry Shiner's 'The Concept of Secularization in Empirical Research', in the *Journal for the Scientific Study of Religion* (Vol. 6, No. 2, 1967, pp. 207–20) remains a landmark essay. If you are digging around in journals, then see Richard Fenn's 'The Secularization of Values: An Analytical Framework for the Study of Secularization', *Journal for the Scientific Study of Religion* (Vol. 8, No. 1, 1969, pp. 112–24).

Still with journals, Joseph Pine and James Gilmore, 'Welcome to the Experience Economy', *Harvard Business Review* (July–August, 1998, pp. 12–25) and Grace Davie, 'Believing without Belonging: A Liverpool Case Study', *Archives de Sciences Sociales des Religions* (38e Année, No. 81, January–March 1993, pp. 79–89) are valuable ports of call. See also Charles. J. Sommerville, 'Secular Society/Religious Population: Our Tacit Rules for Using the Term Secularization', *Journal for the Scientific Study of Religion* (Vol. 37, No. 2, 1998, pp. 249–53).

FROM THE LIBRARIAN: REFERENCES AND FURTHER READING

Peter Berger's *The Desecularization of the World* (Eerdmans, 1999) proclaimed that 'a whole body of literature by historians and social scientists loosely labelled secularization theory is essentially mistaken' (p. 2). Paul Heelas and Linda Woodhead's *The Spiritual Revolution* (Blackwell, 2005), *The Great Dechurching* by Jim Davis, Michael Graham and Ryan Burge (Zondervan, 2023) and Elle Hardy's *Beyond Belief: How Pentecostal Christianity Is Taking Over the World* (Hurst, 2021) all point to decline. The truth for the Western world is that while many are queuing at the front door of Pentecostal churches, significant numbers are also leaving by the back door.

As Galen Watts notes in *The Spiritual Turn* (Oxford University Press, 2022), religion is not disappearing from the landscape so much as being transformed before our very eyes. Robert Fuller's *Spiritual But Not Religious: Understanding Unchurched America* (Oxford University Press, 2001), along with Linda Woodhead and Rebecca Catto's *Religion and Change in Modern Britain* (Routledge, 2012), note the same. The modern world is not secular. It remains spiritual, and with every indication, the effervescence and creativity of spirituality are growing and extensive. However, the outlook for churches and organized religion looks challenging and bleak, and overall forecasts are grim.

Robert Putnam's *Bowling Alone: The Collapse and Revival of American Community* (Simon & Schuster, 2000) and *Our Kids: The American Dream in Crisis* (Simon & Schuster, 2015) note the collapse of voluntary institutions and neighbourly connections, with implied implications for religious patterns of belonging. Putnam charts the alarming acceleration of individualism in American society, laying the foundation for less corporate religious bonding and belief and greater emphasis on personal spirituality. The landscape, then, is changing fast. Just as Robert Bellah noted in his *Habits of the Heart: Individualism and Commitment in American Life* (HarperCollins, 1985). More recently, Charles Taylor's *A Secular Age* (Harvard University Press, 2007) challenged what he called 'the subtraction thesis' – that science leads to religion being subtracted from more and more areas of public life, and so society becomes more secular.

Readers interested in contemporary fusions of the sacred and secular in Christian beliefs and practices have a veritable buffet of options to consider. Cristina Rocha's *Cool Christianity: Hillsong and the Fashioning of Cosmopolitan Identities* (Oxford University Press, 2024) is worth a look, perhaps set against Martyn Percy's, 'Christmas in the Anglican Tradition', in Tim Larsen, ed., *The Oxford Handbook of Christmas* (Oxford University Press, 2020, pp. 153–66), which highlights the secular and cultural influences on Christmastide. Emma Percy's essay in Robert Boak Slocum and Martyn Percy's edited collection, *Fearful Times, Living Faith* (Wipf & Stock, 2021), looks at religious, spiritual and moral themes in *Queer Eye*.

Edward Bailey (1936–2015) was the doyen of these types of engagements and created an entirely new field of academic study. The concept of implicit religion has, since the late 1960s, informed and enriched both theology and the sociology of religion. Bailey was the first to systematically explore and assess the idea that many secular activities have a religious dimension. His *Implicit Religion in Contemporary Society* (Kok Pharos, 1997), *Implicit Religion; An Introduction* (Middlesex University Press, 1998) and 'Implicit Religion' in *The Oxford Handbook of the Sociology of Religion*, ed. P. Clarke (Oxford University Press, 2009) are important landmarks in the field, along with Tim Jenkins' *Religion in English Everyday Life* (Berghahn Books, 1999).

Readings on secularization

I have divided this list into three – Classic (qualitative and quantitative histories and sociology up to 1990), Contemporary (1991 onwards, and around the time when postmodernism and consumerism started to surface as significant interpretative paradigms) and Confessional (i.e. Christian or theological critiques or defences).

This list is by no means exhaustive (that would be a book in its own right), so this is just a sample of the writers that can guide the reader for further study and discussion.

Classic

Peter Berger, *The Sacred Canopy: Elements of a Sociological Theory of Religion*, Doubleday, 1967.
Peter Berger, *The Social Reality of Religion*, Faber, 1969.
Peter Berger et al., *The Homeless Mind*, Penguin, 1974.
Owen Chadwick, *The Secularization of the European Mind in the Nineteenth Century*, Cambridge University Press, 1975.
Harvey Cox, *The Secular City: Secularization and Urbanization in Theological Perspective*, SCM Press, 1965.
Jeffrey Cox, *The English Churches in a Secular Society*, Oxford University Press, 1982.
Karel Dobbelaere, 'Secularisation: A Multi-Dimensional Concept', *Current Sociology*, Vol. 29, No. 2, Sage, 1981.

Mary Douglas, 'The Effects of Modernization on Religious Change, *Daedalus*, Vol. 111, No. 1, Winter 1982, pp. 1–19.
Richard Fenn, *Liturgies and Trials: The Secularization of Religious Language*, Blackwell, 1982.
Richard Fenn, *Toward a Theory of Secularization*, Connecticut University Press, 1978.
Alan Gilbert, *Religion and Society in Industrial England*, Longman, 1976.
Alan Gilbert, *The Making of Post-Christian Britain*, Longman, 1980.
Robin Gill, *Social Context of Theology*, Mowbray, 1975.
Peter Glasner, *The Sociology of Secularization: A Critique of a Concept*, Routledge, 1977.
David Harvey, *The Condition of Postmodernity*, Blackwell, 1989.
Thomas Luckmann, *The Invisible Religion*, MacMillan, 1967.
Alasdair MacIntyre, *Secularization and Moral Change*, Oxford University Press, 1967.
David Martin, *A General Theory of Secularisation*, Blackwell, 1978.
Hugh McLeod, *Religion and the People of Western Europe 1789–1987*, Oxford University Press, 1997.
Edward Norman, *Christianity and World Order*, Oxford University Press, 1978.
William Pickering, *Durkheim's Sociology of Religion*, Routledge, 1984.
Vernon Pratt, *Religion and Secularisation*, Macmillan, 1970.
Larry Shiner, 'The Concept of Secularization in Empirical Research', *The Journal for the Scientific Study of Religion*, Vol. 6, No. 2, 1967, pp. 207–20.
Rob Towler, *The Need for Certainty: A Sociological Study of Conventional Religion*, Routledge, 1984.
Ernst Troeltsch, *The Social Teachings of the Christian Churches*, Macmillan, 1931.
Bryan Turner, *Religion and Social Theory*, Heinemann, 1983.
Bryan Wilson, *Religion in Secular Society: A Sociological Comment*, Watts & Co., 1966.
Bryan Wilson, *Religion in Sociological Perspective*, Oxford University Press, 1982.
Charles Wright Mills, *The Sociological Imagination*, Oxford University Press, 1959.

Contemporary

Alan Aldridge, *Religion in the Contemporary World: A Sociological Introduction* (1st edn 2000; 2nd edn 2007; 3rd edn 2013), Blackwell, 2013.

Callum Brown, *The Death of Christian Britain: Understanding Secularisation 1800–2000*, Routledge, 2001.

Steve Bruce, *Religion and Modernisation*, Oxford University Press, 1992.

José Casanova, *Public Religions in the Modern World*, University of Chicago Press, 1994.

Steven Connor, *Postmodernist Culture*, Blackwell, 2nd edn, 1996.

Grace Davie, *Religion in Britain: A Persistent Paradox* (based on the earlier *Religion in Britain Since 1945*, published in 1994), Blackwell, 2nd edn, 2015.

Grace Davie, 'Europe: The Exception to the Rule?' in *The Desecularization of the World: Resurgent Religion and World Politics*, ed. Peter Berger, Eerdmans, 1999.

Abby Day, *Believing in Belonging: Belief and Social Identity in the Modern World*, Oxford University Press, 2011.

Abby Day, *Why Baby Boomers Turned from Religion: Shaping Belief and Belonging, 1945–2021*, Oxford University Press, 2022.

Kenda Creasy Dean, *Almost Christian: What the Faith of Our Teenagers is Telling the American Church*, Oxford University Press, 2010.

Elizabeth Drescher, *Choosing our Religion: The Spiritual Lives of America's Nones*, Oxford University Press, 2016.

Clive Field, *British Religion and the World Wars: A Subject Bibliography of Modern Literature*, Cambridge Scholars Press, 2019.

Clive Field, *Counting Religion in Britain, 1970–2020: Secularization in Statistical Context*, Oxford University Press, 2021.

Robin Gill, *The Myth of the Empty Church*, SPCK, 1993.

Robin Gill, *The 'Empty' Church Revisited*, Routledge, 2003.

Paul Heelas and Linda Woodhead. *The Spiritual Revolution: Why Religion Is Giving Way to Spirituality*, Blackwell, 2005.

Danièle Hervieu-Léger, *Religion as Chain of Memory*, Rutgers University Press, 2000.

David Lyon, *Postmodernity*, Open University, 1994.

Hugh McLeod, *The Religious Crisis of the 1960s*, Oxford University Press, 2007.

Frank Newport, *God is Alive and Well: The Future of Religion in America*, Gallup Press, 2012.

Pippa Norris and Ronald Inglehart, *Sacred and Secular: Religion and Politics Worldwide*, Cambridge University Press, 2004.

Dylan Reaves, 'Peter Berger and the Rise and Fall of the Theory of Secularization', *Denison Journal of Religion*, Vol. 11, No. 1, 2012, pp. 11–19.

Rodney Stark and Roger Finke, *Acts of Faith: Explaining the Human Side of Religion*, University of California Press, 2000.

Confessional

Paul Avis, *Faith in the Fires of Criticism*, Darton, Longman & Todd, 1995.

Gregory Baum, *Religion and Alienation: A Theological Reading of Sociology*, Paulist Press, 1975.

Harvey Cox, *Religion in the Secular City: Toward a Postmodern Theology*, Simon & Schuster, 1985.

Andrew Greeley, *Unsecular Man: The Persistence of Religion*, Knopf Doubleday, 1972.

Os Guinness, *The Last Christian on Earth* (previously published as *The Gravedigger File*, 1983), Baker Books, 2010.

David Lyon, *Sociology and the Human Image*, InterVarsity Press, 1983.

Eric Mascall, *The Secularisation of Christianity: An Analysis and a Critique*, Darton, Longman & Todd, 1965.

Peter Schmiechen, *Saving Power: Theories of Atonement and Forms of the Church*, Eerdmans, 2005.

Anthony Thiselton, *Interpreting God and the Postmodern Self*, T&T Clark, 1995.

www.ingramcontent.com/pod-product-compliance
Lightning Source LLC
Chambersburg PA
CBHW022221090526
44585CB00013BB/665